Investigating the Mafia

Other titles in Lucent's Crime Scene Investigations series include:

Ballistics
Blackmail and Bribery
Body Farms
The Case of the Green River Killer
The Case of the Zodiac Killer
The Columbine School Shootings
Computer Hacking
The Crime Scene Photographer
Criminal Profiling
Cybercrime
DNA Evidence
Fingerprinting
Forensic Art
Forensic Biology
The Forensic Entomologist
The Homicide Detective
Identity Theft
The John F. Kennedy Assassination
Kidnapping
The Murder of Emmett Till
The 9/11 Investigation
The O.J. Simpson Murder Trial
The Oklahoma City Bombing
Poisoning
Surveillance
Tracking Serial Killers
The Unabomber
Underwater Forensics

Investigating the Mafia

by Carla Mooney

LUCENT BOOKS

A part of Gale, Cengage Learning

GALE
CENGAGE Learning

Detroit • New York • San Francisco • New Haven, Conn • Waterville, Maine • London

LIBRARY OF CONGRESS CATALOGING-IN-PUBLICATION DATA

Mooney, Carla, 1970-
 Investigating the mafia / by Carla Mooney.
  p. cm. -- (Crime scene investigations)
 Includes bibliographical references and index.
 ISBN 978-1-4205-0212-1 (hardcover)
 1. Mafia--United States. 2. Organized crime--United States--History.
 3. Criminal investigation--United States. I. Title.
 HV6446.M66 2010
 363.250973--dc22

                                                        2009040329

Lucent Books
27500 Drake Rd.
Farmington Hills, MI 48331

ISBN-13: 978-1-4205-0212-1
ISBN-10: 1-4205-0212-3

Printed in the United States of America
 2 3 4 5 6 7 14 13 12 11 10

Printed by Bang Printing, Brainerd, MN, 2nd Ptg., 01/2011

Contents

Foreword

The popularity of crime scene and investigative crime shows on television has come as a surprise to many who work in the field. The main surprise is the concept that crime scene analysts are the true crime solvers, when in truth, it takes dozens of people, doing many different jobs, to solve a crime. Often, the crime scene analyst's contribution is a small one. One Minnesota forensic scientist says that the public "has gotten the wrong idea. Because I work in a lab similar to the ones on *CSI*, people seem to think I'm solving crimes left and right—just me and my microscope. They don't believe me when I tell them that it's the investigators that are solving crimes, not me."

Crime scene analysts do have an important role to play, however. Science has rapidly added a whole new dimension to gathering and assessing evidence. Modern crime labs can match a hair of a murder suspect to one found on a murder victim, for example, or recover a latent fingerprint from a threatening letter, or use a powerful microscope to match tool marks made during the wiring of an explosive device to a tool in a suspect's possession.

Probably the most exciting of the forensic scientist's tools is DNA analysis. DNA can be found in just one drop of blood, a dribble of saliva on a toothbrush, or even the residue from a fingerprint. Some DNA analysis techniques enable scientists to tell with certainty, for example, whether a drop of blood on a suspect's shirt is that of a murder victim.

While these exciting techniques are now an essential part of many investigations, they cannot solve crimes alone. "DNA doesn't come with a name and address on it," says the Minnesota forensic scientist. "It's great if you have someone in custody to match the sample to, but otherwise, it doesn't help. That's the investigator's job. We can have all the great DNA evidence in the world, and without a suspect, it will just sit on the shelf. We've all seen cases with very little forensic evidence get solved by the resourcefulness of a detective."

While forensic specialists get the most media attention today, the work of detectives still forms the core of most criminal investigations. Their job, in many ways, has changed little over the years. Most cases are still solved through the persistence and determination of a criminal detective whose work may be anything but glamorous. Many cases require routine, even mind-numbing tasks. After the July 2005 bombings in London, for example, police officers sat in front of video players watching thousands of hours of closed-circuit television tape from security cameras throughout the city, and as a result were able to get the first images of the bombers.

The Lucent Books Crime Scene Investigations series explores the variety of ways crimes are solved. Titles cover particular crimes such as murder, specific cases such as the killing of three civil rights workers in Mississippi, or the role specialists such as medical examiners play in solving crimes. Each title in the series demonstrates the ways a crime may be solved, from the various applications of forensic science and technology to the reasoning of investigators. Sidebars examine both the limits and possibilities of the new technologies and present crime statistics, career information, and step-by-step explanations of scientific and legal processes.

The Crime Scene Investigations series strives to be both informative and realistic about how members of law enforcement—criminal investigators, forensic scientists, and others—solve crimes, for it is essential that student researchers understand that crime solving is rarely quick or easy. Many factors—from a detective's dogged pursuit of one tenuous lead to a suspect's careless mistakes to sheer luck to complex calculations computed in the lab—are all part of crime solving today.

La Cosa Nostra

It was after lunch on a hot and humid summer day in South Philadelphia in 1993. Two friends, Joey Merlino and Mike Ciancaglini, walked down the street toward their clubhouse on Sixth and Catharine streets. Without warning, a car pulled up next to them and shots rang out. Merlino and Ciancaglini fell to the ground. "We both went down together," Merlino explained later. "I knew I wasn't hurt that bad. It looked like he got shot in the arm."[1]

As Merlino crawled over to Ciancaglini, he realized that his childhood friend was in trouble. "I'm dyin',"[2] Ciancaglini whispered to Merlino as blood poured out of his mouth. The bullet had pierced Ciancaglini's heart. Merlino could not do anything. Ciancaglini died that day on the street. "I wish I would've died; he would've lived. I got no kids,"[3] Merlino told Ciancaglini's wife.

Merlino immediately knew who was behind Ciancaglini's murder. That is because Merlino and Ciancaglini were members of the Philadelphia Mafia. Ciancaglini's murder was retaliation for the earlier shooting of Joe Ciancaglini Jr., Mike's brother. With the brothers sitting on different sides of a Mafia power struggle, Mike himself had ordered the hit on Joe Jr. Now one brother was permanently disabled, the other dead.

A Brutal Family

The Mafia that tore apart the Ciancaglini brothers is one of the world's most famous organized crime groups. The American Mafia, also known as La Cosa Nostra, has become part of pop culture for its role in movies and television shows like *The Godfather* and *The Sopranos*.

In real life the Mafia is a brutal group of criminals driven by greed. Frequent power struggles for control plague the Mafia, often ending in death. In order to gain money and power, Mafia members commit many types of crimes. As thieves, they steal truckloads of merchandise to resell. They extort and bribe officials to gain control of labor unions and certain industries like construction and sanitation. They smuggle drugs into cities. They run gambling and loan-sharking operations. For anyone that crosses or opposes them, the Mafia has a violent answer —often murder.

The Mafia uses strict rules and violent punishments to keep its criminal members in line. In the Mafia, violators of the internal code are offered no second chances or jury trials. Punishment is swift and severe. Break a rule and a Mafia man might

Marlon Brando played the role of Mafia boss Don Vito Corleone in the 1972 film **The Godfather.**

find himself looking down the barrel of a gun. He would not be surprised if his best friend, another Mafia man, was the one to lure him to his death.

Hard to Fight

Investigating the Mafia and bringing its criminals to justice is unlike most types of criminal investigations. In a murder or robbery, the investigator focuses on one specific crime. Solve the crime and take the criminal off the street. The Mafia, however, is not a single criminal. Instead it is a group of highly organized criminals that operates like a finely tuned machine. If one part breaks, leaders replace it and the machine continues rolling.

Over the years, law enforcement has found it difficult to stop the Mafia crime machine. Arresting and jailing members for specific crimes is not effective. Instead investigators have the most success when they focus on the organization and not the individual crimes.

A Mafia investigation can be long and tedious. Investigators spend countless hours in surveillance, talking to informants or working in undercover operations. In recent years patience and persistence have allowed investigators to inflict some serious damage to the American Mafia's operations. Despite past successes, investigators know they cannot lessen their pressure on the Mafia. In many ways the Mafia organization is like an out-of-control fire. Tiny sparks constantly ignite new danger spots. "We don't win the war against the Mob," says G. Robert Blakey, author of anti-Mafia legislation. "All we can do is contain or control it."[4]

CHAPTER 1

Knowing the Enemy

What is the Mafia and how does it operate? To investigate the Mafia, law enforcement must first understand it. Organized crime organizations like the Mafia are large, complex groups of criminals. They work together under a set of rules. They follow an established chain of command as if they were military units. The more investigators know about the Mafia, the more likely they are to disrupt its crimes and arrest key players.

Learning about the enemy is called gathering intelligence. Investigators want to know who the key Mafia leaders are and how they operate. They research each person's role in the organization. Investigators are also interested in the relationships among Mafia members. Mafia criminals often fight among themselves and betray each other. Understanding these rifts gives investigators valuable information they can use to place an undercover agent or turn a Mafia member into a police informant. They also learn by studying how the Mafia has evaded law enforcement.

Arrival in America

In the early 1900s Italian immigrants flocked to large American cities like New York, Boston, and Chicago. Most of the immigrants were hardworking, honest people. Some, however, formed criminal gangs. Giuseppe "Joe" Petrosino, a New York City cop in the early 1900s, explained why such gangs were able to thrive: "Here there is practically no police surveillance. Here it is easy to buy arms and dynamite. Here there is no penalty for using a fake name. Here it is easy to hide, thanks to our enormous territory and overcrowded cities."[5]

An Italian immigrant family on board a ferry to Ellis Island, New York, in 1905. Some of the millions of immigrants that passed through Ellis Island's immigration depot would join gangs that would later become the Mafia.

At first the gangs operated independently. Eventually the American gangs realized that by working together they could become more powerful. The organized group would also be harder for law enforcement to track and prosecute.

The gangs formed groups called families. Some families were related by blood, but others were not. Most cities had one ruling family. New York City, because of its size and population, had five major crime families. By the 1930s the new American Mafia was thriving.

Bootlegging Makes the Mafia Rich

In 1920 Congress outlawed the manufacture and sale of all alcoholic beverages. Prohibition, as it was called, helped the Mafia become a rich and sophisticated crime machine. Mafia gangs made liquor in bathtubs or smuggled it into the country from places like Canada, where it was still legal. The Mafia also ran illegal taverns called speakeasies, where people could buy alcoholic drinks. Because people did not stop drinking during Prohibition, the Mafia made millions from bootlegging. "When I first got into bootlegging, I thought it was too good

Roots in Sicily

Sicily is an island in the Mediterranean Sea near the boot tip of Italy. Over its history many foreign countries invaded Sicily and conquered its people. Often the invading governments were corrupt and exploited the Sicilian people. The Sicilians survived these hostile occupations by forming tight alliances with friends and family. These alliances provided safety, justice, and protection. "They are taught in the cradle, or are born already knowing, that they must aid each other, side with their friends and fight the common enemy even when the friends are wrong and the enemies are right,"[1] wrote Louis Barzini, author of *The Italians*.

In this environment a secret society of resistance fighters was born. The Sicilians called it La Cosa Nostra, or "our thing." It would become more widely known as the Mafia. The secret group offered the Sicilian citizens protection from the government for a fee. The group engaged in a vigilante style of justice. English historian Eric J. Hobsbawm explains: "A mafioso did not invoke State or law in his private quarrels, but made himself respected and safe by winning a reputation for toughness and courage, and settled his differences by fighting."[2]

1. Quoted in Selwyn Raab, *Five Families*. New York: St. Martin's, 2005, p. 14.
2. Quoted in Raab, *Five Families*, p. 14.

The tight-knit group Cosa Nostra orginated in Sicily, the island located near the boot tip of Italy.

to be true. I didn't consider it wrong. It seemed fairly safe in that the police didn't bother you. There was plenty of business for everyone. The profits were tremendous,"[6] wrote Mafia boss Joseph Bonanno.

Prohibition bootlegging also taught Mafia gangs how to plan and run complicated operations. They became experts at coordinating the many smugglers, truckers, and gunmen needed for their operations. They learned how to bribe police and politicians to look the other way. Mafia millionaires devised ways to launder money from their illegal operations to make it appear as if they earned it through legitimate businesses. During these years the Mafia evolved from street gangs into sophisticated regional and national crime organizations.

Family Structure

One reason the American Mafia thrived is its strict control over members and their activities. Mafia families are tightly organized groups that operate with high precision. Most families have a similar structure and chain of command.

The head of the family is called the boss. A Mafia member can become a boss by a vote of family members. He can also inherit the position when a previous boss dies of natural causes. Other men, like John Gotti, seize power. Gotti was a capo, or captain, in New York's Gambino family. In December 1985 Gotti organized a hit on Gambino family boss Paul Castellano. Shooters gunned Castellano down in the street as he left a restaurant. After the shooting Gotti called a meeting of the capos in which they unanimously endorsed him to be the next Gambino boss.

A Mafia boss rules the crime family and passes down orders through the ranks. He also settles arguments between family members. The boss earns money by taking a cut from all family moneymaking schemes. Often he invests in a legitimate business to hide the income from his illegal businesses. The boss enjoys money, power, and prestige. This makes him envied by lower family members. It also makes him a target for men like Gotti who are eager to promote themselves.

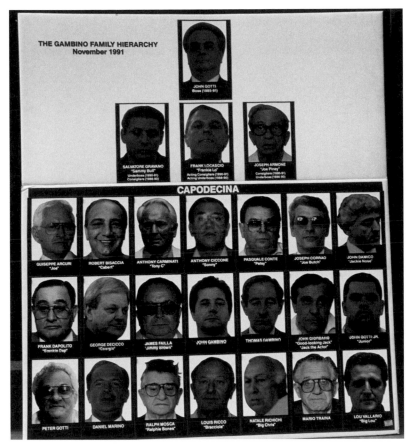

John Gotti became the boss of the Gambino family in December 1985 when he organized a hit on family boss Paul Castellano.

The boss's second in command is the underboss. Most bosses select a trusted ally as their underboss. He usually negotiates disputes and also receives a cut of the family's moneymaking schemes. In some families the boss has another advisor called the consigliere. This is usually an older, wiser member who advises the boss on all matters.

The capos report to the boss and underboss. The number of capos depends on the size of the family. Some families only have a few capos, while others, like the Gambino family, have had more than twenty at one time. A capo is responsible for a small crew of Mafia soldiers and associates. The more money a capo brings in to the family, the more respect and power he gains. The capo takes a portion of the money his soldiers make and passes a portion up to his boss and underboss.

New York's Five Families

In New York City five families emerged as the powerhouses of the American Mafia. The Bonanno, Colombo, Gambino, Genovese, and Lucchese families sliced up the city into five territories. They had their fingers in countless businesses and industries. In fact, by the 1970s most New Yorkers did not pass a single day without using something that the Mafia controlled.

At its height in the mid-twentieth century, the New York Mafia collected a tax on many basic goods like clothing, food, and gas. They had interests in the fish, beef, and poultry markets and also controlled grocery stores. When eating in New York, a meal's price most likely included a tax to one of the five families. Shoppers paid a similar tax on clothing. Most clothing sold in the United States passes through the New York City garment center, and the Mafia controlled the trucking that transported the clothes. Mafia payments inflated trucking fees. If a clothing designer refused to pay the tax, no other trucking company would take the designer's clothes. Beyond food and clothing, New York's five families controlled commerce at the New York ports and the sanitation industry. They also collected lucrative payoffs and kickbacks from city construction companies and a percentage of all concrete contracts.

Mafia soldiers carry out the orders of their capos. "The soldiers in a family are the entrepreneurs who make money and who pay taxes to their bosses. In return they expect the bosses to give them the right to conduct businesses in certain areas and to have disputes among themselves and other families settled peacefully,"[7] said Ronald Goldstock, director of the New York State Organized Crime Task Force.

Being a Mafia soldier is an honor in the criminal world. Mafia soldier Tony Accetturo remembered how he felt during his induction: "I was bursting with excitement. It was the greatest honor of my life. They set me apart from ordinary people. I was in a secret society that I was aching to be part of since I was a kid, from the time I was a teenager."[8]

In addition to initiated members, Mafia families have many associates. These men and women take part in criminal activities under a Mafia member's guidance and supervision. Some associates help unload hijacked trucks or fence stolen goods. Other people help the Mafia operate as well. Crooked cops ignore Mafia operations. Corrupt politicians steer lucrative city contracts to Mafia-controlled businesses in exchange for bribes.

Other associates have a more violent role. Ex-con and mob associate Willard Moran accepted a five-thousand-dollar assignment from the Philadelphia mob to murder rival John McCullough. Near Christmas 1980 Moran dressed as a deliveryman and arrived at McCullough's home with flowers. As McCullough talked on the phone, Moran shot and killed him with bullets to the head and body.

Becoming a Made Man

Becoming a member of a Mafia family is called "being made," "getting your button," or "getting straightened out." The prospective member must have a father with Italian heritage. Some families require both parents to be of Italian descent. In addition, the Mafia is still an all-boys club. Women cannot become members.

At first a capo sponsors the prospective member. Before the induction, the new man must prove himself worthy. This usually means that he has to participate in a murder. He might not be the actual shooter but should be willing to pull the trigger if necessary. Mobster Joseph Valachi proved himself by renting an apartment for his Mafia friends to spot an assassination target. When the target was successfully killed, Valachi earned his ticket into New York's Lucchese family.

The time and place of a man's induction into the Mafia is a closely guarded secret. Often he does not even know it is going to happen until the day his capo tells him to "get dressed." Hearing those words, the man knows his induction is about to take place.

The capo takes his man to the induction's designated place. Because the meeting is top secret, the men are careful to make sure no one, especially law enforcement, follows them. They might switch cars in an underground garage or drive in circles for hours before taking several sharp turns to lose any followers.

In a typical induction ceremony, the prospective member arrives with his capo at the secret location. There a group of men awaits. In a 1989 Boston ceremony secretly taped by the Federal Bureau of Investigation (FBI), the induction began with the leader speaking in Italian: "In onore della Famiglia, la Famiglia e abbraccio," which means, "In honor of the Family, I embrace the Family."[9] The inductee then swore, "I . . . want to enter into this organization to protect my family and to protect all my friends. I swear not to divulge this secret and to obey, with love and omerta [oath of secrecy]."[10]

After the oath the men lead the prospective member to a ceremonial table. They use a needle or knife to prick the man's finger and drop his blood onto a picture of a saint. The man lights a match and burns the paper in his hand. As it burns, the man repeats another oath, "As burns this saint so will burn my soul. I enter alive into this organization and leave it dead."[11]

Most associates want to become made men. Once made, a man receives more respect and earns more money. Mafia members introduce each other as *amico nostro*, or "a friend of ours." This signal shows the made man can be trusted to hear family secrets.

Once a man is chosen for induction, however, there is no turning back. Refusal to participate in an induction ceremony

By the Numbers

3,000

Number of made men in America in 2009

is a death sentence. The refusing man is branded an informant for another family or the police and killed immediately.

Living by the Rules

Once inducted into the Mafia, a man follows a strict code of rules. These rules help the Mafia keep their organization's activities secret and running smoothly. Men obey the rules because they know that those who disobey will receive swift and severe punishment, even death.

One of the most important Mafia rules is *omerta*, the code of secrecy and silence. "To betray the secret of the Cosa Nostra means death without trial,"[12] warned Mafia boss Salvatore Maranzano at Joseph Valachi's induction. *Omerta* keeps members silent, even if they have to do jail time themselves. In addition, if another family murders a mafioso, the family does not report the crime to the police. Instead they handle justice and revenge themselves.

For many years *omerta* insulated Mafia bosses from prosecution. If no one spoke about their involvement in a crime, the underlings' crimes could not be linked to the bosses.

Another important rule is that the member must place the Mafia family first in his life. He must answer the call of his family before all else, including God, his wife, and his children. He must obey all orders from his superiors. If ordered to kill, the member must carry out the murder even if the target is a close friend or family member.

If a member disobeys orders, he may be killed. Louis Di-Bono was a soldier in New York's Gambino crime family. When family boss John Gotti ordered him to a meeting to discuss business deals that had gone bad, DiBono offered excuses to avoid the meeting. This disobedience marked him for death. "Know why he's dying? He gonna die because he refused to come in when I called,"[13] Gotti explained to another family member. Soon after, DiBono was shot to death.

Rules help the Mafia run like a well-oiled machine. Lower-level soldiers and associates know they need to request permission from their capo before they do anything. This includes all business dealings and even vacations outside of the family's territory. Keeping strict tabs on everyone's movements and activities helps the family prevent conflicts with its other illegal schemes.

Extortion

The Mafia makes money in many illegal ways. The Mafia's criminal activities are called rackets. Because the organization runs the rackets, it is hard for law enforcement to stop them. If police arrest one member, another member takes his place in the operation. The Mafia's illegal rackets continue.

One of the oldest Mafia moneymakers is extortion. In an extortion scheme, the Mafia offers to protect a business in exchange for a fee. Many business owners pay the fee in cash. Others agree to order supplies from a Mafia-owned or Mafia-controlled supplier. Restaurants might hand over weekly fees collected at the restaurant's coat check station.

If a business refuses to pay the protection fee, the owner might be beaten or a fire might mysteriously happen on the property. Jim Turner, an Arizona historian, remembers several bars and restaurants that blew up during the 1960s and 1970s in his hometown of Tucson, Arizona. "We all knew what happened," he said. "The guy [owner] wasn't paying."[14]

Extortion schemes are difficult to stop. Business owners fear retaliation if they complain to the police. In addition, if the police do arrest one Mafia member, another member continues the extortion.

A Long List of Crimes

In addition to extortion and bootlegging alcohol, the Mafia expanded their operations into other crimes. They bootlegged goods like cigarettes and narcotics. During World War II the Mafia sold counterfeit or stolen ration stamps for food, gas, and clothing.

In places where gambling was illegal, the Mafia ran backroom card games and slot machines behind stores and social clubs. They also ran numbers games similar to the lottery. They

In an extortion scheme, the Mafia collects money from businesses in exchange for protection. When an owner refuses to pay, his or her business might be burned to the ground by the Mafia.

fixed sporting events by bribing boxing competitors or horse trainers and jockeys. They offered protection to brothels and other houses of prostitution for a fee. The Mafia loan sharks also lent money to people in need. They charged extremely high interest rates on their loans. Debtors who did not pay back the loan on time risked life and limb.

Today's Mafia runs many rackets, including theft, extortion, drug trafficking, gambling, labor racketeering, loan sharking, prostitution, pornography, tax-fraud schemes, and stock manipulation schemes.

Labor Racketeering

Labor unions are another source of the Mafia's money and power. The Mafia infiltrates and manipulates unions in order to control the union's businesses and industries. Often Mafia racketeers extort or bribe union officials. They offer favorable contracts or settle disputes in exchange for the union accepting their demands.

Former Gambino family boss Paul Castellano said in the 1980s, "Our job is to run the unions."[15] His words rang true in 1986, when the President's Commission on Organized Crime reported that the Mafia controlled five major unions, including the Teamsters and the Laborers International Union of North America.

According to the FBI, labor racketeering costs Americans millions of dollars each year. When it controls a union, the Mafia sets pricing in the union's industry. Consumers pay more money for goods made with inflated labor costs. The Mafia may also organize strikes and work slowdowns in order to keep its hold on labor rackets.

Union members suffer from the Mafia's labor racketeering. The ultimate prize for Mafia racketeers is getting control of the union's health, pension, and welfare funds, many of which are worth billions of dollars. According to the U.S. Department of Labor, there are "millions of dollars of workers' dues and benefit monies that have been siphoned off by organized crime through embezzlement or more sophisticated devices such as fraudulent loans or excessive fees paid to corrupt union and benefit plan service providers."[16]

Bribery

The Mafia recognizes that it would not be able to run its rackets without outside help. Mafia members bribe police, judges, and politicians for their cooperation. Regular bribe payments ensure these officials will keep quiet and leave the Mafia family alone. One of the reasons that the Mafia has flourished is because many of the officials who were supposed to investigate and arrest them were actually paid off by the Mafia.

Camden, New Jersey, mayor Milton Milan walks into court for his trial on November 6, 2000, in which he is accused of accepting payoffs from organized crime figures. The Mafia often pays off the officials who are supposed to investigate and arrest them.

At other times bribes help the Mafia win lucrative contracts or favors. Milton Milan, former mayor of Camden, New Jersey, was convicted in 2000 of accepting Mafia bribes. During Milan's trial, Philadelphia Mafia boss Ralph Natale testified that he gave more than thirty thousand dollars to Milan in the hope that he would grant city contracts to mob-owned businesses.

The Commission

With Mafia families full of criminals, it was inevitable that there would be interfamily disagreements. If the dispute could not be solved, it usually ended in violence. In the early 1900s interfamily wars killed many Mafia leaders. Family bosses recognized that this pattern of violence did not benefit anyone, especially the bosses, who were often targets. In 1931 several bosses met in Chicago. One boss, Lucky Luciano, said, "I explained to 'em we was in a business that hadda keep movin' without explosions every two minutes; knockin' guys off just because they come from a different part of Sicily, that kind of crap was given' us a bad name, and we couldn't operate until it stopped."[17]

By the Numbers

13,075

Number of FBI special agents as of March 2009

The bosses decided to form a group that would act as the governing body for the American Mafia. They called this group the Commission. At first the Commission had seven members. Each of the five major New York crime families had a seat, along with representatives from the Chicago and Buffalo families. Smaller families from other parts of the country were assigned to one of these seven men to represent their interests. In 1961 the Commission expanded and added two additional members.

The Commission acts as a link among the American Mafia families. It sets policies and procedures for all families. It settles any disputes. The Commission also provides cooperation for joint family ventures.

The Mafia's Impact

With the Commission in place, the Mafia was able to become bigger, richer, and more powerful than ever. By the 1960s a Justice Department analysis estimated that the Mafia's illegal profits were equal to that of the country's ten largest industrial corporations combined. That list included giants like General Motors, Standard Oil, Ford Motors, U.S. Steel, and IBM. Today the FBI estimates that global organized crime nets more than $1 trillion annually.

All that money helps the Mafia extend its reach and influence. Mafia groups manipulate financial markets, labor unions, and industries like construction and sanitation. They smuggle drugs into cities. They endorse a culture of violence as they extort, intimidate, and murder to keep their operations rolling.

The American Mafia is an efficient criminal machine. Because there are so many tentacles and layers of members, law enforcement often finds it difficult to dismantle the machine. Arresting and jailing one member for a specific crime does little to stop a family's rackets. A new member steps into place and the Mafia's crimes continue.

CHAPTER 2

Mafia Fighters

Investigating the Mafia is more than solving an individual crime like a robbery or murder. Instead investigators focus on the Mafia organization behind the crimes. Some investigations take years to gather enough evidence to arrest key mobsters. As a result, Mafia investigations are long and expensive. "You can't bring the mob to justice unless you are willing to devote a significant amount of time and money to long-term, proactive investigations that may in the end fail to reach any conclusive results,"[18] said prosecutor John Kroger.

During a long investigation, a team of professionals works together to dismantle Mafia organizations and put mobsters behind bars. The team members come from a variety of agencies. They have different skills, each of which is an important part of bringing down the mob.

FBI Special Agents

The spearhead of most Mafia investigations is the FBI. The FBI has a special division called the Organized Crime Section that targets Mafia criminals. The FBI has field offices across the country. Each field office investigates Mafia activity in its area. A special agent in charge, or supervisor, leads the office's organized crime squad. In New York City the FBI organized crime unit is divided into five family squads. Each squad focuses on one of the five major New York crime families. FBI headquarters in Washington, D.C., coordinates and supports the investigations of its field offices.

All special agents begin training at the FBI Academy in Quantico, Virginia. For twenty-one weeks, trainees study investigative subjects in class. Out of the classroom, trainees push their bodies to the limit in physical fitness training. They learn defensive tactics and practice shooting firearms. They also practice strategies for field operations like raids, arrests, and surveillance. If the trainees pass all tests and complete all training requirements, they graduate from the academy. They are then sworn in as special agents.

New special agents are assigned to an FBI field office. Some report to the organized crime squad. There they learn about the Mafia organization and activities in the territory. "Upon arriving at the Buffalo office of the FBI and reporting to the organized-crime squad . . . I spent the first several weeks reviewing seven years' worth of intelligence files, focusing on mob activities,"[19] said former FBI special agent in charge Joe Griffin.

For FBI special agents every day is different. One day they might testify in court. The next day they could stake out a target and photograph everyone they meet. Successful special agents combine the street smarts of big-city cops with the FBI's

Agents from the Federal Bureau of Investigation (FBI) and New York City police detectives escort alleged Mafia members out of a booking facility.

Becoming an FBI Special Agent

Job Description:
An FBI special agent is responsible for conducting national security investigations and enforcing federal statutes. FBI special agents work many cases, including terrorism, foreign counterintelligence, cybercrime, organized crime, white-collar crime, bribery, bank robbery, extortion, and kidnapping.

Education:
A prospective FBI special agent must have a four-year college degree and three years of professional work experience. They must also be citizens of the United States or its territories.

Qualifications:
Candidates first complete an online application. Qualified applicants are then selected for Phase I testing, a series of written tests. If the candidates pass Phase I testing, they move on to Phase II testing, which is another written test and an in-person interview. Upon passing Phase II, the candidate undergoes a series of fitness and medical tests and a background investigation. If all tests are passed, the candidate attends a twenty-one-week special agent class at the FBI Academy. The academy provides classroom learning and intense physical training. Candidates learn defensive tactics, practical application exercises, and firearms use. Upon successful completion of the training program, candidates are sworn in as FBI special agents.

Salary:
The salary for a trainee at the FBI Academy starts at $51,000. New special agent salaries range from $61,000 to $70,000.

investigative techniques. Agents gather intelligence by watching mob targets and listening to wiretaps. They review surveillance tapes and identify incriminating sections. They read thousands of old and current reports on suspects. When prosecutors need more evidence to support their case, it is the special agent's job to find it.

Special agents maintain general intelligence files on Mafia targets. "People call the FBI with tips like 'Joe Mobster will be at a certain restaurant at 2 P.M. on Saturday' or 'There's a new capo in town,'"[20] said former New York prosecutor Ellen Corcella. General information helps agents identify which suspects and places to investigate. A tip about an upcoming meeting might help them know where to plant electronic bugs or position a surveillance team.

Agents and Informants

Another important part of a special agent's job is developing and managing informants. "To successfully investigate the Mob it is absolutely essential to have a few good, solid informants helping you out. You can't really do much without the informants. That's one of the first steps in starting a successful investigation. Without well-placed informants, an investigator is in the dark,"[21] said former special agent Joe Griffin.

Sometimes agents will knock on a mobster's door and hand him a business card. "Call me sometime," the agent will say. Two years later the agent might get a call when the mobster is in trouble and sees informing as a way out.

At other times agents develop informants from previous investigations. When Griffin investigated the Cleveland crime family, he identified a potential informant who had worked with a retired agent. Griffin thought the man could be a valuable source of information again. He decided to pay him a visit. Griffin recalled:

I drove out to his house. Still an active bookmaker, he was not exactly delighted to see me. But after we talked for a while, he soon realized that if his prior relationship with the FBI was renewed, he could breathe a little easier in his own bookmaking business, even if it meant putting his life on the line for the FBI. . . . After I secured his trust, this informant provided a great deal of previously unknown information.[22]

To develop informants, FBI agents will sometimes contact a mobster and hand him his information, hoping to get a call years later when the mobster is in trouble.

Developing informants is one of the most difficult parts of a special agent's job. Griffin explains:

> Developing and operating an organized-crime infor-mant is an extremely dangerous but absolutely essen-tial activity. There is a fine line you must walk—you are dealing with a criminal, knowing he is committing crimes that you must overlook for the greater good. An agent must secure the trust of the informant, but he or she has to be extremely careful not to get too close to the informant. Many agents never develop infor-mants because of the fear of getting into trouble, but these are not successful agents and they are not doing their job. . . . I have never seen an excellent agent who did not have good informants.[23]

Working with Other Agencies

FBI agents also work on task forces with detectives from state and local police forces. Many big-city police forces have an or-ganized crime unit. Their detectives gather intelligence on lo-cal Mafia families. In an investigation the FBI and the police might split up the detective work. While FBI agents monitor a wiretap, police detectives might get a search warrant and con-duct a raid to look for guns, stolen goods, or drugs.

At times the FBI and police detectives may need to work with other agency investigators. For example, if a Mafia in-vestigation involves a hijacking from New York's John F. Kennedy airport, they might call agents from the U.S. Cus-toms Service. If an investigation uncovers mail fraud, the U.S. Postal Service joins the team.

Because of the large number of Mafia criminals in the state, New York has its own task force. The Organized Crime Task Force investigates and prosecutes organized crime in the state. According to the task force's Web site, it specializes in "iden-tifying emerging and existing organized crime enterprises and, through a broad array of civil and criminal enforcement techniques, seeks to undermine their structure, influence and presence within the State."[24] The Organized Crime Task Force collaborates with agencies like the FBI and local police for long-term investigations.

Calling in the Specialists

Most Mafia criminals are extremely careful about surveillance. They refuse to use phones to discuss sensitive information. They travel complicated routes to make sure no one is following them. In these cases the Mafia team calls in surveillance specialists.

These agents in the FBI's Special Operations Division conduct surveillance with electronic bugs, cameras, video, and other technical equipment. The surveillance might be fixed, so that agents monitor one location for a period of time. At other times surveillance agents follow a suspect wherever he or she goes. Either way the surveillance work is very time-consuming. Different agents rotate in eight-hour shifts so that the target or location is watched around the clock. They take notes, photographs, and videos to document where the target went and whom they met.

Surveillance technical teams install electronic bugs. They secretly gain access to a location and quickly place the recording equipment. Then they disappear without leaving any traces that would arouse their target's suspicions. Their secretive techniques are kept under tight cover by the FBI. "No one really knows how they got the bug on John Gotti,"[25] said former prosecutor Ellen Corcella.

Sometimes investigators call in translators or language specialists. For a Mafia investigation these specialists are usually fluent in Italian. They analyze any written or audio evidence in Italian. They sort through hours of taped conversations and

By the Numbers

56

Number of FBI field offices

An agent surveys suspicious activity. Surveillance is the most common method for learning about alleged mobsters.

mountains of documents, searching for information that will be important to the investigation. Sometimes they can also recognize and translate coded words or cryptic remarks made by a suspect. "I always have documents or audio materials relating to court cases and investigations to translate," said one specialist, describing her job. "But it's really the unpredictable that's predictable. I can be called on at any moment to translate for a U.S. official . . . or accompany a Special Agent to conduct an interview."[26]

Sometimes traditional techniques are not enough to catch a mobster. In these cases investigators might turn to the accountants for help. Because mobsters make their money illegally, many try to launder it through legitimate businesses. In the process they often fail to report their income to the government and pay taxes. That is where a forensic accountant can help an investigation. Accountants review tax records, bank accounts, loan-sharking ledgers, and many other financial documents to look for incriminating evidence. "One of the best ways to hurt them is in the pocketbook,"[27] said Supervisory Special Agent Nora Conley, who investigates the Bonanno family.

Apalachin Conference

In 1957 it was rumored that an Italian organized crime group was active. Many people did not believe it existed. That changed in November 1957 in Apalachin, New York. Police sergeant Edgar D. Croswell noticed more than a dozen unfamiliar cars gathering at Joseph Barbera Sr.'s home. Because Barbera was a known bootlegger with an arrest record, the gathering aroused Croswell's suspicions.

Croswell returned with more police the next day. They blockaded the road outside Barbera's house. When the men at Barbera's house spotted the police, they tried to leave in a hurry. The police detained forty-six men for questioning, some of them caught while running through the woods to escape.

When the police checked the detained men's identification, they found a who's who cast of Mafia heavyweights. Family leaders like Vito Genovese, Carlo Gambino, Paul Castellano, and Joe Bonanno all attended the Apalachin gathering. The Commission had called the unscheduled meeting to reassure mob families after the recent murder of mobster Albert Anastasia.

Without evidence of a crime, the police released the detained mobsters. Their meeting, however, confirmed the existence of a national criminal organization. Public pressure resulted in law enforcement devoting more time and energy to Mafia investigations.

Bringing Down Big Joey Massino

In the late 1990s investigators had tried almost every technique to bring down New York's Bonanno family boss Joseph "Big Joey" Massino. Two years of work failed to find anything they could use to build a case against Massino. Then they decided to bring in the accountants. Investigators thought that if they could trace how the money was flowing to Massino, they might find a weak spot in Massino's armor. "It's impossible to change records in the banking system. If we had someone who knows what to look for, where the money is going, and how it got there, we might unlock Massino's empire,"[28] said Jack Stubing, the FBI special agent in charge of the Bonanno squad.

Two special agents, Jeffrey Sallet and Kimberly McCaffrey, joined Stubing's team. They were both accountants prior to joining the FBI. Sallet and McCaffrey subpoenaed financial records and combed through thousands of documents. Eventually they identified a lower-level mob associate, Barry Weinberg, who had a parking lot partnership with Massino. They suspected Weinberg might be a weak link. For over a year FBI agents tailed Weinberg. They watched him meet with mobsters and reviewed his bank and financial records. After a year agents were able to link him to tax evasion and other financial crimes. When confronted with the accountants' evidence, Weinberg decided to cooperate with investigators. He gave information to the FBI about years of Bonanno family fraud and payoffs.

With this information, the agents convinced lower-level mobsters to cooperate and inform against their superiors. Eventually they reached one of Massino's capos, who agreed to testify against his boss. This led to Massino's arrest in 2003. He was convicted of many charges, including conspiracy to commit

By the Numbers

0

Number of FBI agents assigned full-time to investigate organized crime during the Mafia's heyday in the 1940s

murder, racketeering, and extortion. For his crimes Massino was sentenced to life in prison.

Capone and the IRS

Another infamous mobster, Al Capone, was also brought to justice by accountants. In the 1920s Capone and his men terrorized Chicago. They were involved in crimes from gambling and bootlegging to robbery and murder. Despite their efforts the police were unable to stop Capone.

Although Al Capone committed violent acts, it was tax evasion that eventually landed him in prison.

Treasury Department agents tried a different approach. They interviewed Capone's accountants. Treasury agents took an inventory of his possessions. Eventually they discovered evidence that Capone had made millions of dollars through his illegal activities. He had not paid a dime of taxes on it. The Treasury agents arrested Capone on tax evasion charges. He was sentenced to eleven years at the Alcatraz federal prison.

J. Edgar Hoover and the FBI

For most of his forty-eight-year reign as FBI director from 1924 to 1972, J. Edgar Hoover refused to acknowledge the existence of the Mafia. He even banned the use of the word *Mafia* in internal reports. Hoover stated that organized crime was a local police problem, not the responsibility of the FBI. Instead Hoover preferred to focus on kidnappers, bank robbers, spies, and suspected communists. He forbade his agents from working undercover to expose illegal operations because he feared it would taint his agency.

Without the attention of Hoover and the FBI, the Mafia's operations were free from significant interference for many decades. Competing agencies like the Treasury Department compiled more information and expertise on Mafia criminals. By 1961 evidence had mounted to support the existence of a national criminal organization. The current attorney general, Robert F. Kennedy, declared a war on the Mafia. He ordered Hoover to investigate more than eight hundred suspected mobsters. Finally the FBI became more involved in the fight against the Mafia. After an initial learning curve, the FBI eventually became one of the most respected law enforcement agencies investigating Mafia crimes in the United States.

Forensic Labs

At a Mafia crime scene, investigators use forensic specialists and crime labs to process any physical evidence. Crime labs identify the remains of Mafia murder victims and report on the cause of death. They comb the crime scene to look for any physical evidence like fingerprints, bullet casings, or fibers. Because mobsters are professional criminals, it is often difficult to find physical evidence of their crimes. Most of the time they carefully dispose of bodies where they may never be found. Mobsters know to wipe down surfaces to remove fingerprints and any other physical traces that might lead back to them.

Sometimes, however, a mobster slips up and leaves a piece of evidence for the forensic team to find. After Bonanno boss Carmine Galante's murder, police found the shooters' getaway car. Forensic tests lifted a partial palm print from the interior. For years the FBI was unable to match the print to any suspect. When they developed a system for identifying partial prints, agents decided to test the forensic evidence again. They ran suspect Anthony "Bruno" Indelicato's complete handprints through the forensic system. It matched. "Bingo, we have him. We nailed him from a left palm print on the inside of one of the doors,"[29] said agent Pat Marshall. Indelicato's handprint would later prove to be an important piece of evidence in the government's trial against the Commission leaders.

Prosecutors

While investigators gather evidence, prosecuting attorneys organize it into a case against the Mafia. Prosecuting attorneys might work for a district attorney's office, a U.S. attorney, or a state attorney general. During the investigation, prosecutors help agents obtain search warrants and court approvals for surveillance requests. As the prosecutors review the evidence, they work with investigators to identify weak spots and brainstorm ways to fill in the holes.

Prosecutors also interview witnesses. They make deals with informants facing prison time. Former assistant U.S. attorney Ellen Corcella dealt with many Mafia informants during her years prosecuting the mob. She would tell them: "After you're done with all your testifying, we'll tell the judge you've cooperated fully. He'll decide if he wants to be lenient on your sentence."[30]

Cooperation Is Key

In a Mafia investigation, cooperation among investigators and agencies is critical. For many years different agencies often worked against each other. They did not share resources or information. Distrust between the FBI and local police hindered Mafia investigations. Today, however, Mafia investigators cooperate more than ever. State investigators help the FBI on Mafia cases. Many local police detectives work full-time with the FBI on Mafia investigations.

Cooperation brings results. In 2008 investigators announced a major bust of the New York Mafia. Fifty-seven mobsters were arrested. The arrests included twenty-five members of the Gambino family and all of its active leadership. This significant bust could not have happened without the efforts of many investigators and agencies. Queens County district attorney Richard A. Brown explained: "Today's arrests were the result of a coordinated law enforcement effort involving a multitude of agencies at all levels of government. The cooperative efforts of the agencies represented here today were critical to ensuring the successful outcome of this major takedown of individuals associated with organized crime. I commend all those who participated in this endeavor."[31]

CHAPTER 3

Surveillance

Surveillance is the starting point of a Mafia investigation. Agents spend hours watching suspects and following their movements. They can also use high-tech surveillance methods like wiretaps, electronic and computer bugs, and video cameras to monitor suspected criminals and listen in on their conversations. Investigators hope patient watching and listening will provide important clues that will lead to a Mafia arrest.

Watching and Waiting

Physical surveillance is one of the primary duties of Mafia investigators. They spend hours watching known Mafia hangouts, looking to see who enters and exits. They take hundreds of photographs, showing different mobsters and associates. A photograph of two mobsters together can later become important evidence to prove their connection. Watching a suspect over a long period helps investigators establish a pattern of activity. Any variations from that pattern could provide important clues to the mobster's illegal activities. Surveillance also verifies tips from informants, proving that the information they pass along is reliable.

Mafia social events like weddings and funerals are great places to gather information about the family structure. Agents often stake out these events. They photograph guests arriving and leaving. They write down guests' license plate numbers and trace the owners. Investigators also try to obtain a guest list or gift list. Under Mafia social customs, the more expensive a gift, the more important the mobster is. "It is amazing what we learned at these functions. You could pretty much determine what rank a man held in the organization by observing his body language and how these individuals interacted with each other,"[32] said former FBI special agent Joe Griffin.

A surveillance agent must have an enormous amount of patience. "Every day you just get a little piece of the puzzle; you don't have to get the puzzle all in one day," said a member of an FBI surveillance group. "It's like something builds up to a very long story, if you will, like a soap opera more so as opposed to a cut-and-dry short story. . . . And you build on it every single day."[33]

Agents who spend a lot of time in surveillance often get to know their target's habits and characteristics. FBI agent Charlie Muldoon was one of the surveillance agents assigned to New York's Gambino family boss John Gotti. "You could just tell by his body language and the way people related to him whether he was in the middle of a crisis. John Gotti's tell was that when he used to get mad, he used to talk a lot more with his hands; he used to be very, very physical with his hands,"[34] Muldoon said.

Following funeral services in February 2001, pallbearers carry the coffin of former Mafia boss Anthony Giacalone. Many believe Giacalone knew the secret behind the disappearance of alleged informant Jimmy Hoffa.

On the Road

Sometimes investigators will follow or tail suspects in a car to see where they are going and whom they plan to meet. Many Mafia criminals drive defensively to escape tails. They exit the highway unexpectedly or pull onto the side of the highway for a few minutes. They might make an abrupt U-turn in the middle of a busy city street.

To counter these techniques several experienced agents usually staff the surveillance squad. Sometimes they buy or rent a variety of vehicles like sports cars or delivery trucks for surveillance. The team's vehicles alternate tailing the suspect. A supervisor talks to each car via radio and tells agents where the suspect is and when they need to drop in and out of the lead position.

Blending In

For FBI surveillance agents, the most important part of the job is to blend in. If they do their job right, no one notices them. "When a target comes out . . . with a cup of coffee, they don't see where we are, or they don't see our people. Our people look so ordinary, they just look over them,"[35] said Todd Letcher, special agent in charge of New York's FBI Special Operations Division. Sometimes the team will plant a man that looks like a cop to attract the target's attention. Focused on the suspected cop, the target might miss the other people on the surveillance team.

To blend in, surveillance agents dress the part. Some agents carry entire wardrobes in their cars. That way they can quickly change into a business suit for Wall Street or athletic shorts for Central Park. Other agents carry bicycles in the car trunk so they can impersonate a New York messenger.

In a typical surveillance assignment, the team first spreads out. "We usually key on something, whether a bright color she [the target] has on or a particular item that might be unique," an unnamed agent said. "We relay that to other team members

Other Mobs

When talking about organized crime, most people think about the Italian Mafia. The Italian Mafia, however, is not the only group of organized criminals. Mobs exist around the world in many different cultures and countries.

The Yakuza are an organized crime group in Japan. Their name comes from the worst possible score in a Japanese card game and is symbolic of being without value in society. The Yakuza trace their beginning to the seventeenth century, making them older than the Sicilian Mafia.

The Russian Mafia came into power when the Soviet Union fell in the 1990s. During the following economic disaster, government workers, KGB agents (the Russian equivalent of the Central Intelligence Agency), military veterans, and others turned to crime. The Russian Mafia spread throughout the world during widespread emigration in the 1990s. In the United States the Brighton Beach neighborhood in Brooklyn became a gathering place for the Russian Mafia.

The Chinese mob, known as the Triads, began as a secret society in the 1800s to battle a corrupt Chinese government. Their crimes include drug dealing, prostitution, gambling, robbery, and murder. One of their major moneymakers is producing counterfeit goods like clothing, coins, computer software, handbags, music, CDs, and movies.

Three Japanese men show off their tattoos, a symbol of membership in the Yakuza, an organized crime group in Japan.

so they can see her when she comes to the next corner, so they would be able to identify her."[36]

The teams have many techniques for following a target. In one technique called leapfrog, an agent follows the target to a certain point, then passes him or her off to another agent. The first agent then leapfrogs ahead to pick up the target further down the street. "They [the agents] should be telling us the next movement, so you don't have to run and pullback, and run and pullback," said an unnamed agent. "That's kind of obvious, especially if there is a possibility that someone could be watching you from the rear."[37]

Picket Surveillance

Surveillance specialists might use this picket surveillance technique to follow a Mafia target walking down the street:

Members of the surveillance team take their positions in the area where the target is moving. Each team member covers a specific street corner or subway entrance.

The first team member identifies the target and selects a distinctive characteristic like a red sweatshirt to make spotting easier. The agent radios this information to the other team members.

As the target passes through a team member's assigned area, the agent carefully watches his or her movements, noting where the target goes, what he or she does, and with whom he or she speaks.

The surveillance agent radios the target's position ahead to other team members. As the target moves, the surveillance agents take turns watching the target as he or she passes through each team member's assigned area.

Team members document information obtained during the surveillance for general information or investigation files.

Wiretaps

Electronic surveillance is one of the most effective ways to gather evidence against the Mafia. By recording Mafia members as they talk about their crimes, agents can use mobsters' own words against them as evidence in a court trial.

Wiretapping is one type of electronic surveillance. It allows investigators to listen in and record a target's phone calls. Before digital telephones, investigators tapped physically into the target's phone line. Investigators installed an electronic wiretapping bug along the phone line. Many times investigators hid the bug directly in the phone's handset. Once investigators installed the bug, they did not have to return to the location.

A bug used power from the phone line to transmit a radio signal for several blocks. The investigators set up a listening site to receive the signal, sometimes in an apartment or van. When the target used the phone, the bug transmitted the conversation to the listening site. There investigators listened and recorded the target's conversations.

With the introduction of digital telephones, wiretapping has become much simpler for investigators. After obtaining a court order to tap a target's phone, investigators contact the phone or communications company. The phone company creates a digital copy of every call that comes through the tapped phone line. They also record information such as the phone numbers at each end of the call and how long each call lasts.

When a wiretap is in place, it is difficult for the target to know someone is listening to his or her conversation. If unsuspecting targets talks about crime details on the tapped phone, investigators will have evidence to use against them in court. Unfortunately, many Mafia members know about wiretaps and refuse to use telephones for sensitive conversations. Lefty Guns Ruggiero, a member of the Bonanno family, once advised undercover FBI agent Joseph Pistone: "When you talk on the phone, you don't talk direct about what's going on. You talk

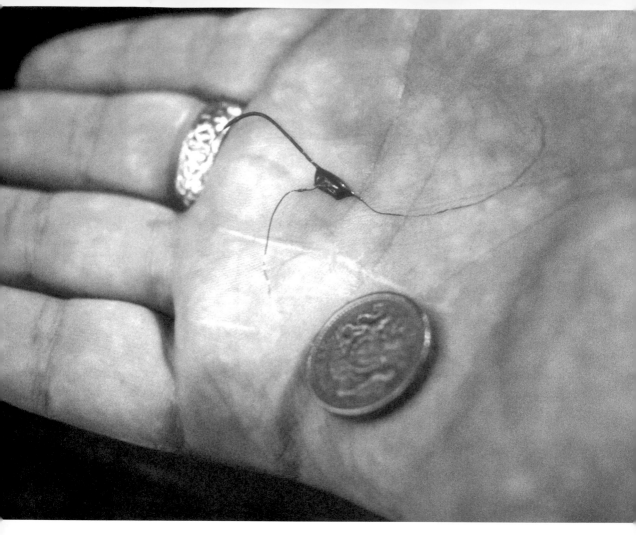

around it, throw me a curve—just give me a hint about what you're talking about. Because all the phones are tapped, you know."[38]

Electronic Bugging

In addition to wiretaps, investigators use small electronic bugs to record mobsters talking in their hangouts. The first electronic bugs that were small enough to be hidden appeared in the 1950s. Law enforcement almost immediately put them to use. Investigators now place bugs in homes, restaurants, and even cars, wherever they suspect a mobster discusses his criminal affairs. To install an electronic bug, agents secretly gain access to the location and plant the device where mobsters will not see it.

Over time, investigators have become expert at hiding bugs. Sometimes they plant bugs in unusual places like stuffed animals, binoculars, or a horse's saddle. Agents have also bugged Roman Catholic churches where mobsters attend services—planting bugs in confessionals, church candlestick holders, and the church bathroom.

A Rainy Night

Sometimes investigators have to work in less-than-perfect conditions to plant a bug. In 1983 two agents for the New York State Organized Crime Task Force rehearsed the planting of an electronic bug. The target was a black Jaguar owned by Lucchese mobster Salvatore Avellino. Family boss Anthony "Tony Ducks" Corallo often traveled in the car. Investigators believed they could obtain valuable evidence from his car conversations with Avellino.

On the night the bug operation was scheduled, a heavy rain blanketed the area. Undeterred, the agents moved forward with their plan. They carefully entered the car in a restaurant parking lot and spread a plastic sheet to protect the seats from the rain. They quickly removed the dashboard, installed the bug, and wiped away any trace of their entry into the car.

The Jaguar bug proved to be a major part of the investigation against the Mafia Commission leaders. For months the bug relayed conversations between Corallo, his driver, and other passengers in the car. "It was the most significant information regarding the structure and function of the Commission that has ever been obtained from electronic surveillance," said Ronald Goldstock, chief of the Organized Crime Task Force.

Quoted in Ed Magnuson, "Hitting the Mafia," *Time*, June 24, 2001. www.time .com/time/magazine/article/0,9171,145082,00.html.

Planting Bugs at Casa Storta

In 1982 the FBI was watching Gennaro "Gerry Lang" Langella, the underboss of New York's Colombo family. On many nights Langella visited a Brooklyn restaurant called Casa Storta. He always sat at a reserved table, far away from other diners.

When the restaurant closed to diners each night, Langella and his mob friends remained at his table and received fresh food from the chef. Agents determined that Langella was using the restaurant to conduct business. They decided to place a bug to see if they could catch him in any incriminating conversations.

One night at 3 A.M., a team of agents arrived at the restaurant to place the bugs. They picked the locks and turned off the alarm system. The agents were careful not to damage the locks so that no one would suspect there had been a break-in. Once inside the restaurant, technicians installed electronic microphones and transmission cables behind the ceiling panels over Langella's regular table. At the same time, other agents patrolled the area outside the restaurant. If someone approached, they could warn the inside agents about the intruder.

During the job the agents ran into one problem—a guard dog. Thinking on their feet, they quieted the dog with blasts of foam from a fire extinguisher.

After placing the bugs, the FBI set up a listening station in a nearby apartment. There they were able to gather evidence and new leads as Langella and his associates ate and talked freely.

Big Paul's House

At other times, getting access to plant bugs is more difficult. In the 1980s Paul "Big Paul" Castellano was the head of New York's Gambino family. Investigators were having a hard time getting any information on him. He did not regularly visit a

By the Numbers

15

Number of minutes it took agents to install an electronic bug in a Mafia boss's car

Paul Castellano, or Big Paul, the reputed former boss of the Gambino family, arrives at federal court for arraignment in 1985. Informants reported that Big Paul often conducted business in his own home to avoid surveillance.

social club or restaurant that they could bug. His phone calls were closely guarded, and wiretaps provided no evidence. Informant reports told the FBI that Big Paul used his own home to conduct business, often sitting at his kitchen table.

Agents used evidence from wiretaps and bugs of other Gambino family members to get legal permission to bug Big Paul's home. The problem, however, was getting inside to plant the bugs. Eight-foot walls (2.4m) circled the property. The main building was protected with burglar alarms, sensors, and closed-circuit video cameras. Floodlights shone over the grounds, and two Doberman pinschers guarded the property. To make matters even more difficult, Big Paul never left his home empty; someone was always in the house.

Agents realized that sneaking in to Big Paul's home would be impossible. Instead they devised a plan to send a disguised agent in broad daylight. In March 1983 agents cut off Big Paul's cable television service. Then an agent disguised as a cable repairman arrived to repair the lines. After several visits to solve cable and phone-line malfunctions, the agent succeeded in placing tiny electronic microphones and wires in Big Paul's house.

The bugs transmitted Big Paul's conversations with his Mafia soldiers to a nearby rented apartment, where the FBI had set up a listening station. In one recording, agents listened to Big Paul complain about the Sparks restaurant, which was not paying his extortion fees. "You know who's really busy making a real fortune? . . . Sparks. I don't get 5 cents when I go in there. I want you to know that. Shut the house this way if I don't get 5 cents,"[39] he warned. This and other recordings from Big Paul's house would eventually become evidence in several Mafia prosecutions.

Problems with Bugs

Sometimes bugs do not work as planned. Background noise from refrigerators, radios, televisions, or air conditioners can cover the target's conversations. When agents first listened to recordings from the bugs in Big Paul's house, for example, they

could not get a clear transmission because of the constant noise of a nearby television and radio. Specialized technicians wiped out the background noise and enhanced the conversation for listening agents.

At other times the target discovers the bugs and either stops talking or removes them. As mobsters become well informed about electronic surveillance, many perform sweeps of their hangouts for bugs. Bonanno family boss Joseph Massino regularly searched for bugs in his club. One day a newly planted bug in his club stopped transmitting. FBI agents suspected that Massino's men had found the bug and ripped it out. James Kallstrom, the Special Operations Division chief, decided he wanted the expensive equipment back and ordered an agent to get it. When the agent tried to sneak in to the club, Massino discovered him and guessed why he was there. "We found it the

In another type of surveillance, investigators can remotely activate a cell phone's microphone, which allows them to listen to any conversation within hearing distance of the phone.

first day. Why didn't you just call, I'd have brought it to you,"[40] he laughed.

Even when the bugs work properly and clearly transmit the mobster's conversations, investigators might have a hard time understanding what they are saying. Older mobsters often speak Italian. In addition, mobsters who have known and worked with each other for years do not recap an ongoing topic. At other times mobsters who are careful about being overheard might speak in code. To help solve these problems, investigators use translators and informants to decode the recorded conversations.

Computer and E-mail Surveillance

As communication technology has evolved, so have the methods investigators use for electronic surveillance. Investigators use special software to monitor mobsters' computer activity. The software is installed at the Internet service provider. It sifts through millions of e-mail messages, looking for e-mails sent by the target. Investigators also ask Internet service providers to conduct wiretaps on computer traffic for mobsters under investigation. This type of surveillance takes place inside the Internet service provider's network at a router, or switch. It can record all Internet traffic, including Web browsing, or only certain types of traffic like e-mail.

Investigators can also capture a mobster's computer activity in other ways. Technicians can sneak a program onto the computer that will take pictures of the monitor. They can also use a hidden camera to capture images on the screen. A system called TEMPEST detects electromagnetic energy from a computer screen. A van parked outside the mobster's house can use that information to re-create computer images. Agents can also secretly plant a device in a computer or

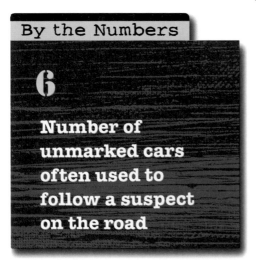

By the Numbers

6

Number of unmarked cars often used to follow a suspect on the road

keyboard that records the suspect's every keystroke.

This was the case after investigators following New Jersey mobster Nicodemo Scarfo Jr. hit a roadblock. Using traditional computer surveillance techniques, they had watched Scarfo's computer communications. They found, however, that he had encrypted all of his sensitive business information. Agents could not break the encryption. They needed Scarfo's password.

So, after getting court approval, FBI agents sneaked into Scarfo's business and planted a keystroke logger in his computer. When Scarfo typed the password into his computer, the agents hit the jackpot. With the password, they were able to decrypt Scarfo's coded files. They used the evidence they obtained to prosecute Scarfo for gambling and extortion.

Microphones and Wires

Another type of electronic surveillance called a roving bug uses the target's cell phone. First, investigators remotely activate a cell phone's microphone. They can then use it to listen in on any conversations within hearing distance of the phone. Once the microphone is switched on, the cell phone sitting on a desk or table becomes a powerful, undetectable bug.

Another option is for an agent to wear a wire. This is helpful with suspects who are wary of talking on the phone or in places where electronic bugs can be hidden. Some suspects prefer to walk and talk outside. In these situations a hidden wire might be the only way to record their conversation. A mole or informant hides the recording device underneath or on his or her clothes. The wire transmits the conversation to listening agents.

Wearing a wire, however, is risky. Some mobsters routinely check associates to see if they are hiding a wire. When FBI agent Joseph Pistone was working undercover as mob associate Donnie Brasco, he deliberately chose not to wear a wire on many occasions. That decision saved his life several times. One time a mob associate came up behind him in a bar. While saying hello, the man ran his hand down Brasco's back. Later that same night, Brasco ran into the man again in the bathroom. This time the man quickly patted down the sides of Brasco's jacket. "I knew what he was doing. He was checking me for a wire,"[41] said Pistone. If he had been wearing one that night, Pistone most likely would have been killed.

Is It Legal?

Electronic surveillance in all forms can provide investigators with invaluable information about crime families and their illegal operations. For many years, however, this evidence was not admissible in court. In 1934 Congress passed the Federal Communications Act. This legislation prohibited the use of wiretaps. Three years later the Supreme Court ruled in several cases to ban the use of evidence from electronic surveillance. In 1939 Attorney General Robert Jackson directed the FBI not to use wiretaps.

Even though they could not use the evidence in court, investigators continued to use electronic surveillance for decades to gather information. Finally, in 1968 Congress relented and passed the Omnibus Crime Control and Safe Streets Act. Within the act, a section called Title III permitted the use of electronic surveillance.

To use evidence obtained from electronic surveillance in court, investigators follow strict procedures. Agents must demonstrate that all other intelligence-gathering techniques have already been tried. They show probable cause that the target has committed or is planning crimes. Investigators show why they believe the bug or wiretap will provide evidence of a crime. They also show that the location or phone to be bugged has been used in past criminal activity and may be used in the future. To meet these conditions the investigator gathers evidence from informants or other surveillance.

Once an investigator is ready to request the bug, he or she files an application with a judge. If the judge approves the electronic surveillance, the investigator has thirty days to bug or wiretap the target. At the end of the thirty-day period, the investigator can apply for an extension if he or she can prove that more evidence is likely to follow.

Electronic surveillance has become one of the most valuable tools in a Mafia investigation. According to investigators and prosecutors, it is very hard for defendants to overcome the evidence this surveillance provides. Many prosecutions of Mafia criminals have been successful because of wiretaps and electronic surveillance.

CHAPTER 4

Inside Information

Some of the most important evidence gathered in a Mafia investigation comes from people on the inside of the organization. Sometimes the inside information comes from family members themselves. They may be trying to get revenge or save their lives. Whatever the reason, these informants turn on their family and cooperate with investigators. At other times the insider is an undercover investigator who works his way inside a Mafia family.

Informants

Informants are a necessary part of a Mafia investigation. They live in the underworld and secretly pass information to investigators. Most informers do not talk solely to help investigators. They want something in return. Some talk to earn goodwill with law enforcement. They believe if they are arrested in the future, they might be treated leniently. Alternatively, investigators might not look too closely at their nonviolent crimes, like bookmaking. Other informers decide to turn, or become informants, when facing significant prison time. They hope that by cooperating and providing information on the family, their sentence may be reduced.

A typical informant might be a low-level Mafia associate who is busted for his crimes. To shorten his prison time, the associate makes a deal with investigators. He promises to inform on his Mafia contacts and bosses. He provides information about the people and illegal activity that he knows. Based on his information, investigators arrest higher-level Mafia members. They lean on these men, trying to convince them to inform on their superiors. If investigators can keep turning the next layer of Mafia criminals, eventually they can reach high into the organization.

While investigating the Colombo crime family, FBI agent Seamus McElearney convinced several mobsters to become informants. In one case, he remembers, "this individual was able to realize that he'd be going away for the rest of his life, and like anything in life, you build a rapport with someone, and you have to get over that trust factor. And he started to trust me and realize this was his best option."[42]

A bookie takes note of a bet. Informants often cooperate with the police to obtain leniency for non-violent crimes, such as bookmaking.

Joe Griffin, a former FBI special agent, developed informants by aggressively investigating and arresting Mafia members and associates. "We also capitalized on outstanding intelligence info we received from the microphones and other sources to zero in on the weaknesses within the . . . family structure."[43] Once the target was arrested, Griffin placed pressure on the potential informant to convince him to turn.

Evaluating Informant Information

Informants give investigators tips on where mobsters will be, what they are doing, and whom they are meeting. "If you've groomed an informant . . . , he will tell you that they are either planning future crimes, engaged in ongoing crimes, or bragging about past crimes,"[44] said Griffin. Using this information, investigators can set up surveillance teams.

Despite their help, informants are criminals first. Sometimes informants try to trick agents by passing only trivial information or tips that turn into nothing. In one case Neil Welch, FBI assistant director in New York City, remembers an informant who passed information that purposely misled the FBI. "It was the Mob's version of what they wanted us to know and we weren't going out there, investigating, doing any real work to find out if it was fact or fiction,"[45] said Welch.

Breaking *Omerta*

By talking, an informant breaks the Mafia's vow of silence, *omerta*. The Mafia warns members and associates to keep quiet. During an investigation of the Mafia in Newark, New Jersey, a mob thug warned city contractor Paul Rigo to "keep your mouth shut and remember you have a pretty daughter."[46] Later, Rigo found a note in his car. The chilling message read: "This could have been a bomb. Keep your mouth shut."[47]

If family members suspect someone is talking to the police, the consequences are serious. The suspected informant can be punished by death, even if the charges are never proved. In 1990 Alphonse D'Arco, the acting boss of the Lucchese crime family, called in Louis "Louie Bagels" Daidone. "Bruno Facciola is a rat,"[48] D'Arco said. The family wanted Facciola killed, and Louie Bagels was given the murder contract. He and two associates lured Facciola into a garage. There Louie Bagels stabbed and shot him in the head and eyes. He then stuffed a dead canary into Facciola's mouth. The message sent was, "You sing to the feds, you're going to get your head blown off."[49] Ironically, Facciola had not talked to the feds at all.

Joseph Valachi

One of the most famous mob informants was Joseph Valachi, a soldier in New York's Genovese crime family. Before he testified in October 1963, many people denied that the Mafia existed. Valachi's testimony, broadcast on television and radio, changed that forever. He was the first Mafia member to acknowledge publicly that the Mafia existed. William Hundley of the U.S. Justice Department explains:

> What he did is beyond measure. Before Valachi came along, we had no concrete evidence that anything like this actually existed. In the past, we've heard that so-and-so was a syndicate man, and that was about all. Frankly, I always thought a lot of it was hogwash. But Valachi named names. He revealed what the structure was and how it operates. In a word, he showed us the face of the enemy.[50]

While serving time for a narcotics conviction in 1962, Valachi landed in the Atlanta prison that held family boss Vito Genovese. During their time together, Valachi became convinced that Genovese thought he was an informant. Valachi recalled: "One night in our cell Vito starts saying to me, 'You know, we take a barrel of apples, and in this barrel of apples there might be a bad apple. Well, this apple has to be removed, and if it ain't removed, it would hurt the rest of the apples.'"[51]

Other Mafia inmates also began to avoid Valachi. Before long, Valachi feared he was marked to die. On June 22, 1962, Valachi

Joseph Valachi, one of the most famous Mafia informants, takes an oath before testifying on mob activity in September 1963.

thought the hit was coming. Fearing for his life, he grabbed an iron pipe and beat to death an inmate that he suspected was the hit man. Unfortunately for Valachi, he killed the wrong man.

The FBI believed that the killing was a turning point for Valachi. One special agent of the FBI said: "Valachi has no real remorse for anything he has done in his life, except this. Nothing crushed him more than the fact that he got the wrong man. It really plagues him. Getting a guy who was going to get him was the one satisfaction he was willing to settle for. If he had been successful, he probably never would have talked."[52]

Now Valachi faced a murder charge. When he learned that prosecutors were going to ask for the death penalty, Valachi reached out to the government. He wanted to cooperate. In return, he was able to plead guilty to murder in the second degree. Valachi avoided the death penalty and instead received a life sentence.

To interview him, the government flew Valachi to the Westchester County Jail near New York City. They separated him from other prisoners to keep him safe. At first Valachi was reluctant to talk, but FBI agent James P. Flynn gained his trust and confidence. Once talking, Valachi answered all of the investigator's questions. He talked about his entire thirty-year history with the Mafia. Valachi explained the Mafia's organizational structure and initiation ceremonies. He named bosses and other members. He explained the roles of each person in the organization and how orders are followed.

Like many informants, Valachi was still a violent criminal. He did not talk to perform a good deed. "Revenge was a large part of it, but it was also a cold, calculated move for survival. Don't think for a moment that this was a repentant sinner. He was a killer capable of extreme violence. He was devious, rebellious against all constituted authority, and he lived in a world of fear and suspicion,"[53] said Flynn.

Although his testimony did not lead to the arrest of many Mafia leaders, it provided invaluable information. Valachi's testimony also encouraged the government to increase the money and agents they devoted to investigating the Mafia.

Sammy the Bull Gravano Talks

Although Valachi may have been the first public Mafia informant, he was certainly not the last. For years Gambino boss John Gotti evaded law enforcement. He escaped conviction in the 1980s and 1990s through witness intimidation and jury tampering. His nickname, Teflon Don, grew because prosecutors were unable to make charges against him stick. That changed when trusted underboss Salvatore "Sammy the Bull" Gravano turned informant.

In 1990 the FBI once again arrested Gotti, along with Gravano. Gotti probably fully expected to beat the charges as he had in the past. This time, however, investigators had a recording of Gotti admitting to three murders. In the tape he blamed Gravano for instigating the murders. When agents played the tape for Gravano, he believed Gotti might turn on him in court. He decided it was time to save himself.

Gravano had his wife contact the FBI. In a secret meeting, he agreed to cooperate. At first investigators were surprised. Gravano was the last person they expected to turn. "It's unheard of. The underboss of a major family testifying against his boss? Is he for real, or is this some kind of setup manipulated by Gotti?"[54] asked U.S. attorney Andrew Maloney.

Despite the investigators' initial concerns, Gravano did not waver from his decision to break *omerta*. He provided investigators with full details about the Gambino family and their criminal activities. On March 2, 1992, he took the witness stand against his boss, John Gotti. To a shocked courtroom, Gravano stated, "I was the underboss of the Gambino organized crime family. John was the boss; I was the underboss. John barked and I bit."[55]

Gravano testified for nine days. His testimony and the electronic recordings of Gotti himself were unbreakable in court. On April 2, the jury returned its verdict. Gotti was guilty of racketeering and murder. He was sentenced to life in jail.

The government knew that such an explosive witness was in danger of being killed in a Mafia hit. To protect him, they

kept him separated from other prisoners. While he was in court, the government surrounded the building with U.S. marshals. They also placed SWAT team agents in the courtroom.

Over the next few years, Gravano testified in other Mafia trials. His information helped send many criminals to jail. Gravano's testimony was a serious crack in the Mafia tradition of *omerta*. He showed how even a high-ranking mobster could save his own skin and start a new life. It created a serious drop in morale. Bosses and capos around the country wondered who in their organization they could trust.

In return for his cooperation, Gravano received a five-year sentence. For a man who had committed at least nineteen murders

Salvatore "Sammy the Bull" Gravano, former member of the Gambino family, broke **omerta** *and testified against his boss, John Gotti, in 1992. Gravano testified in other Mafia trials and helped send several criminals to jail.*

and countless other crimes, it was a bargain. "He got the deal of a lifetime. Using some of these guys is like taming a wolf. You can feed them out of your hand but they're still wolves, and you can never trust them. Sammy was in that category,"[56] said Bruce Mouw, a former FBI agent.

Even though he helped prosecutors put away dozens of criminals, Gravano himself could not turn away from crime. After his release from prison, he settled with his family in Arizona under a fake name. Within a few years he and some of his family were caught dealing drugs. Gravano was sentenced to twenty years in prison.

A Mole in the Family

Working with informants can be tricky. Sometimes investigators have to make a deal with one criminal in order to bring down another one who is worse. At other times informants appear untrustworthy in court, and their testimony is useless. Ralph Natale, apparent boss of the Philadelphia crime family, successfully testified against crooked politician Milton Milan. When he took the stand in mobster Joey Merlino's trial, however, the result was different. It was clear to the jury that Merlino had orchestrated Natale's rise to boss and that Merlino was the one who controlled the family. At the trial the jury discounted Natale's testimony against Merlino. "The feds fell in love with the idea of flipping a boss before they found out he was a paper boss. He came across as a pompous ass who was repeating a lot of stories he had heard, not someone who lived them,"[57] said George Anastasia, Philadelphia mob expert. As a result, the jury acquitted Merlino on several charges, including murder. He received a light sentence of only fourteen years for gambling and extortion.

Some investigations use a more reliable source for inside information than informants—undercover agents, or moles. FBI agent Joseph Pistone, who worked undercover as a Bonanno family associate, explains: "Informants are valuable but unreliable. They are crooks buying their life-style or freedom

Keeping Clear Undercover

Working as an undercover agent against the Mafia can be extremely difficult. Joseph Pistone, who spent six years undercover, explains:

All the guys around you have Caddies and pinkie rings and broads and cash, and it's easy to forget that you're not one of them. If you don't have a strong personality and ego, a sense of pride in yourself, you're going to be overcome by all this, consumed by the role you're playing. The major failure among guys working undercover for any law-enforcement agency is that they fall in love with the role. They become the role. They forget who they are.[1]

An undercover agent lives in a criminal world and pretends to be part of it. However, he always remembers that his actions will be scrutinized long after the case is over. "When I was undercover, with every step I took I had to think: How will this seem when I testify? I had to be absolutely clean. Money had to be accounted for. I had to document what I could and remember what I couldn't document. Finally it would come down to my word in front of the juries,"[2] says Pistone.

1. Joseph D. Pistone and Richard Woodley, *Donnie Brasco: My Undercover Life in the Mafia*. New York: New American Library, 1987, pp. 98–99.
2. Pistone and Woodley, *Donnie Brasco*, p. 3.

with information, and they may lie or exaggerate to get a better deal. A government agent working undercover, sworn and paid to uphold the law, is more trustworthy, more credible, before a jury. But it's a risky business. You can get dirty, you can get killed."[58]

Working as a Mafia mole is like being a spy. An undercover agent pretends to be a low-level criminal. He takes on a new identity and lives in the undercover world. "You have to be street-smart, even cocky sometimes," says Pistone. "Every good undercover agent I have known grew up on the street, like I did and was a good street agent before becoming an undercover agent. On the street you learn what's what and who's who. You learn how to read situations and handle yourself. You can't fake the ability. It shows."[59]

Over time, the agent works his way around Mafia members and associates. He tries to gain their trust. If the agent is successful, he gathers enough evidence to make arrests. He will testify in court about his undercover operation and help prosecutors win their case against the mobsters. Over the years many government moles have been able to work their way into different mob families. Most keep their success out of the public eye. They fade into the background, sometimes relocating with a new name and identity in order to avoid revenge from the Mafia.

Donnie Brasco

FBI agent Joseph Pistone is one of the most famous former mob moles. Pistone spent almost six years undercover, working as a minor jewelry thief named Donnie Brasco. At first his assignment to bust some major stolen goods fences was to last only a few months. As Pistone worked, he made his way into a Mafia crew. Pistone and his supervisors realized they had an excellent opportunity to take down more criminals.

Over the years Pistone slowly met and gained the trust of several mobsters. They believed he could be a valuable asset to their criminal enterprise. What they did not know, however, is that he was regularly passing information to his FBI supervisors. To fool the mob, Pistone had to think and act like a criminal. He explained: "I maintained a low profile, the way I'm comfortable. I didn't volunteer more about myself than was necessary; I didn't ask questions that didn't need to be asked— even though information I wanted was often just out of reach. But I knew that certain things I did would catch the eye of

THE WAY OF THE

DONNIE BRASCO

AKA JOSEPH D. PISTONE
AUTHOR OF THE *NEW YORK TIMES* BESTSELLER *DONNIE BRASCO*
INCLUDES CD WITH FBI SURVEILLANCE AUDIO FROM THE DONNIE BRASCO OPERATION

The cover of The Way of the Wise Guy, *a book by Joseph D. Pistone about his six years as an FBI undercover agent inside the Bonanno crime family.*

people or have people talking. I had to be patient, just let things develop."[60]

Living as Donnie Brasco was hard. Pistone had to lie constantly and think on his feet to maintain his cover. He also spent years separated from his family and friends, with only occasional secret visits home.

Life undercover was dangerous. One wrong step and his cover could be exposed. If the Mafia had discovered Pistone was an undercover FBI agent, he would have been killed immediately. Only a few people in the FBI knew about Pistone's assignment. Even his family did not know that he was working undercover against the Mafia.

Most of the time, Pistone did not wear a wire out of fear of being discovered. He also was afraid to make written notes in case his person or apartment was searched. Instead Pistone memorized his information and passed it to the FBI on a regular basis.

Pistone's undercover work provided a mountain of information to the FBI. He discovered inside information on the Bonanno family and the Mafia in general. He identified the leaders, what crimes they were involved in, and how they operated the family. In the end, Pistone's evidence led to more than one hundred federal convictions.

In 1981 the FBI decided to close down Pistone's operation. He had risked his life for six years and provided invaluable information. Now it was time for him to get out. In July 1981 FBI agents visited mobster Dominick "Sonny Black" Napolitano, who had worked closely with Brasco. The FBI told Napolitano that Brasco was really an undercover FBI agent. Pistone had done his job so well that at first Napolitano did not believe them.

By the Numbers

$500,000

The amount of the Mafia murder contract on undercover agent Donnie Brasco

News of Brasco's operation caused uproar in the Bonanno crime family. Men blamed for bringing Brasco into the family were killed or kicked out. A few weeks after the FBI met with Napolitano, Bonanno leaders summoned him to a meeting. It was the last time he was seen alive. Mafia leaders also put out a murder contract on Donnie Brasco. When the FBI got wind of the contract, they visited the leaders of each of the five New York crime families.

A Mole in the FBI

Sometimes the mobsters get their own valuable inside information. In the Cleveland FBI office, informants tipped off agents that the Cleveland family was getting information on FBI investigations from someone on the inside. They gave agents a list of informants that they said came from the mob mole. When agents verified that the list was accurate, they knew that they needed to find out who was leaking information.

They assembled a small group of investigators on a highly confidential basis. The team planted fake information in the organized crime files. They quietly installed hidden cameras in the FBI office. They also planted an undercover agent to pose as an office clerk.

The break came when investigators found FBI documents at a mob-affiliated car dealership. Handwritten notes on the list had distinctive little o's instead of dots over the letter i. Agents immediately recognized the handwriting as that of Geraldine Rabinowitz, a longtime FBI employee and trusted clerk.

When confronted with the list, Rabinowitz broke down and confessed. She and her husband had become affiliated with a local mobster and were slowly drawn in to helping him. For their crimes, Rabinowitz and her husband were sentenced to five years in prison.

"Hands off this agent, he beat you, it's finished,"[61] they warned. If Brasco was hurt, agents promised that the full fury of the Justice Department would come down on the Mafia families.

After the operation Pistone began a new chapter with his family. "At forty-eight, I will begin a new life under a new name. Except for close friends and some government officials, no one will know that I am the man that lived this life as Joe Pistone and Donnie Brasco,"[62] he said.

CHAPTER 5

RICO and the Law

Since 1970 new laws have made it easier to investigate and arrest Mafia criminals. The most important of these laws, the Racketeer Influenced and Corrupt Organizations (RICO) statute, allows investigators to arrest anyone who is part of a conspiracy to commit a crime. If an investigator can prove a suspect is connected to and has helped an organization like the Mafia commit a crime, then the suspect can be arrested. For the first time investigators could charge Mafia bosses in connection with the crimes of their capos, soldiers, and associates.

RICO

In the 1960s law enforcement recognized that an arrest of an individual, low-level Mafia member had little effect on the Mafia as a whole. If a member went to jail, the Mafia family substituted members in his place and continued its criminal activities. Additionally, investigators had a hard time convicting the bosses of any serious crimes. A boss might order a murder, but often little evidence connected him to the crime.

In 1970 Congress armed investigators and prosecutors with new legislation designed to convict Mafia criminals and dismantle their organization. The most powerful of these laws was the RICO statute, part of the Organized Crime Control Act of 1970. RICO took aim at organized crime and punished those convicted with serious jail time and hefty fines.

When investigators build a RICO case, they try to prove suspects have engaged in a pattern of racketeering as part of a criminal enterprise. The RICO statute lists more than thirty

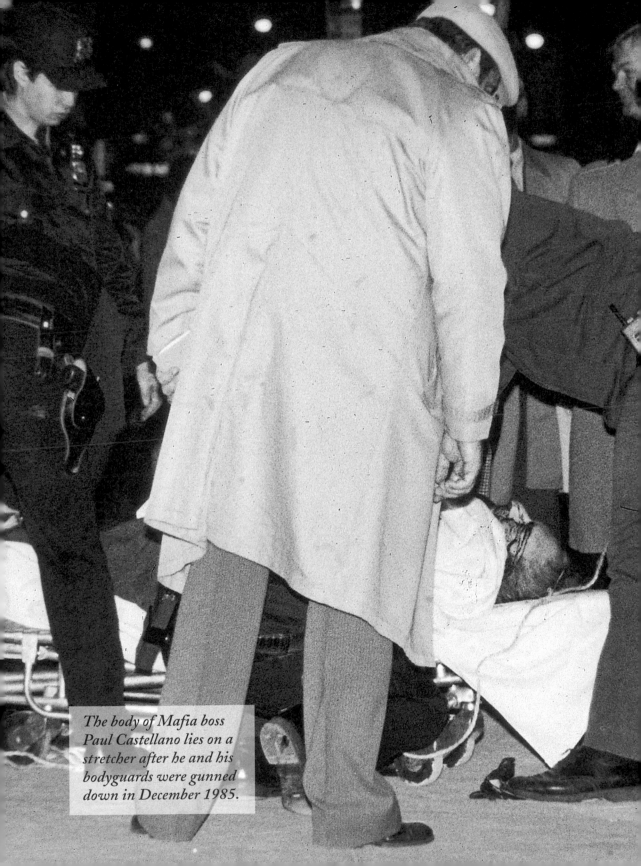

The body of Mafia boss Paul Castellano lies on a stretcher after he and his bodyguards were gunned down in December 1985.

different crimes, such as extortion, bribery, loan sharking, murder, drug dealing, money laundering, kidnapping, arson, and robbery. If an organization commits two or more crimes from the list, these acts become a pattern of racketeering.

In Mafia investigations the criminal enterprise is the Mafia family. Before RICO, prosecutors could not mention a defendant's past crimes. Now prosecutors can introduce a defendant's previous crimes to prove he is a member of a Mafia family.

The Man Behind RICO

G. Robert Blakey had his first exposure to the Mafia while working as an attorney for the Department of Justice's Organized Crime and Racketeering Section. After four years in the section, Blakey became a law professor at Notre Dame in 1964. There he developed a popular course on organized crime. In 1966 Blakey agreed to become a consultant for a federal task force analyzing organized crime. While working with the task force, Blakey began to develop a legal plan to bring down the Mafia.

Blakey recognized that existing laws did not effectively combat the Mafia's system of organized crime. Instead of individual crimes, Blakey began to think about laws to bring down the larger organization. He realized that making it illegal to run a criminal enterprise was the key. Law enforcement would be better able to reach insulated mob bosses. In addition, heavy prison time and financial penalties would give prosecutors a sharper bite. Stiff penalties coupled with a new witness protection program could convince key players to testify against the Mafia.

By 1968 Blakey had joined with Senator John McClellan to get his ideas written into law. With McClellan's support in Congress, Blakey's RICO statute became law as part of the Organized Crime Control Act of 1970.

Using RICO, investigators can arrest Mafia bosses and other members even if they personally did not bribe, kill, or extort victims. With informant testimony and evidence from electronic surveillance, prosecutors can show that crimes by low-level associates were a pattern of racketeering for the benefit of the Mafia family. Evidence that the boss received a cut of illegal money or talked about arranging the family's activities is enough to link him to the crimes. In addition, anyone in the family who receives or gives a report about a family crime can be convicted. Under RICO the Mafia boss and other leaders are no longer protected.

Heavy Penalties

Not only does RICO allow investigators to prosecute more Mafia criminals, it also hands out heavy penalties to those convicted. Before RICO most Mafia criminals convicted of individual crimes only served a few years in jail. They did their time, got out, and resumed their criminal activities. Now a single RICO conviction carries a prison term of up to twenty years. If murder is one of the crimes, the defendant can receive life in prison.

The RICO laws also hit the Mafia's wallet hard. A defendant convicted under RICO can be fined $250,000 or twice the proceeds of the crime. The defendant must also forfeit any proceeds he has earned from the criminal enterprise. The government can seize the mobster's assets, including his home, property, and bank accounts. These penalties can financially wipe out convicted mobsters and seriously damage the Mafia's ability to finance new operations.

Focus on the Organization

For RICO to be most effective, investigators focus on the criminal enterprise, not a specific crime or criminal. In a RICO case, investigators build one piece of evidence upon another. "Don't pull a bug after you get confirmation and evidence for one easy conviction. Climb the ladder until you get to the top of the organization,"[63] said G. Robert Blakey, creator of the RICO statute.

Investigators can use evidence from the first wiretap to get another. Each piece builds a stronger case against the Mafia family. "If you uncover evidence of a homicide, make the fact of the murder an item of evidence," said Blakey. "Show a series of homicides and other crimes and you've proven the acts of racketeering. Demonstrate the existence and pattern of an enterprise and connect the murders and other crimes, and you've got a RICO indictment and almost certain conviction."[64]

Protecting Witnesses

Investigators knew that they also needed a way to protect witnesses who testified against the Mafia. Violent Mafia criminals routinely killed or intimidated witnesses to prevent them from testifying. Witness killing also sent a message to others to keep their mouths shut. Frank Balistrieri, a Milwaukee Mafia boss, once said, "No witness ever lived to testify against me."[65]

By the Numbers

78 PERCENT

Percentage of cases using the Witness Security Program that produces convictions

In 1970 Congress established the Witness Security Program. The program is run by the U.S. Marshals Service, part of the Justice Department. Federal agents protect witnesses and their families before and during the trial in which they will testify. After the trial witnesses and their families relocate to an unidentified area. They get new names, social security numbers, job histories, and school records. The program supports witnesses in their new location for about a year, until they get a job and establish a new life. Witnesses cannot contact anyone from their old life. In the case of an emergency, the witness has a phone number to call a U.S. marshal.

The Witness Security Program is not perfect. Although witnesses are expected to live a law-abiding life after relocation,

James Cardinali was a key witness at the 1987 trial of reputed boss John Gotti and later dumped by the Witness Security Program. Cardinali believes he is now an easy target for organized crime members.

some revert to their criminal ways. In those cases they risk being kicked out of the program. In addition, the promise of a new life away from prison tempts some criminals to lie on the witness stand.

New Laws Crack *Omerta*

Omerta, the long-standing Mafia code of silence, protected mobsters for years. Without witnesses, investigators found it difficult to link bosses and capos to crimes they ordered and directed. The Witness Security Program and the stiff jail time under RICO convictions, however, have become strong tools for investigators to crack the *omerta* code.

Most mobsters were willing to do a few years in jail for various crimes. They knew their Mafia family would be waiting for them when they returned. However, long RICO sentences have changed many attitudes. Some decide that decades or even life behind bars is too high a price to pay for the family. They decide to look out for themselves and try to cut the best deal they can with the government.

The fear of retaliation also was a powerful deterrent against mobsters turning informant. The promise of protection in the Witness Security Program, however, helped ease fears. Now investigators can convince more mobsters to talk.

Angelo Lonardo Turns Witness

Shock waves rippled through the American Mafia when a Cleveland family acting boss testified before a Senate subcommittee in 1988. The man stated: "My name is Angelo Lonardo. I am 77 years old, and I am a member of La Cosa Nostra. I am the former underboss of the Cleveland organized crime family. I became a member of La Cosa Nostra in the late 1940s but have been associated with the organization since the late 1920s. My father, Joseph Lonardo, was the former boss of the Cleveland family."[66] With Lonardo's words the code of *omerta* was shattered.

RICO penalties and the Witness Security Program provided investigators with the keys to breaking Lonardo's loyalty to his

Mafia family. In April 1983 prosecutors convicted Lonardo of RICO racketeering and drug charges. The seventy-two-year old Lonardo received a sentence of life plus 103 years. Six months into his hefty RICO sentence, Lonardo decided to cooperate with investigators and turn informant. The thought of dying in jail did not appeal to the mob boss. "I know I will never get out of there alive, and I miss my family very, very much,"[67] he told a Senate subcommittee.

Lonardo knew that if he broke the rule of *omerta*, he would be a target for Mafia killers. He asked investigators if they could protect him and place him in the Witness Security Program. When they agreed, Lonardo opened up about Cleveland's mob activities and his connections with other bosses and families.

The testimony he provided was an important part of convictions in mob cases across the country. During his debriefing and trial testimony, FBI agents guarded Lonardo twenty-four hours a day. In return for his cooperation, Lonardo's sentence was reduced to five years' probation. He also entered the Witness Security Program. Lonardo's case shows how a veteran mobster can be turned into an informant by the promise of reduced jail time and protection.

By the Numbers

$100,000

The cost to the government for each person in the Witness Security Program

RICO and Labor Unions

In April 1985 the chair of the President's Commission on Organized Crime announced that the Mafia dominated several major unions. One of the unions named was the International Brotherhood of Teamsters (also called the Teamsters Union). Corrupt Teamster presidents like Dave Beck and Jimmy Hoffa had served jail time over the years. Their convictions did little to end the Mafia's control over the Teamsters. If a corrupt leader went to jail, a new Mafia-controlled leader took his place.

Jimmy Hoffa, former head of the International Brotherhood of Teamsters. Allegedly the Mafia controlled several major unions, including the Teamsters.

The Mafia's skimming of union workers' wages and benefits continued.

With RICO, however, prosecutors could use the antiracketeering laws to go after Mafia-controlled labor unions. In 1988 the government filed a RICO suit against the Teamsters. They sought to overthrow the eighteen-member Teamster executive board. Since 1970 the government had convicted more than 340 defendants of Teamster-related crimes such as murder, shootings, theft, extortion, and bribery. During those years the board had done nothing to clean up the corruption.

Buffalo Local 210

In 1994 the U.S. government threatened the Laborers International Union of North America (LIUNA) with the same type of RICO case it had filed against the Teamsters. To avoid the suit, LIUNA agreed to clean up the union and remove Mafia influences, particularly at the local level. One of the worst offenders, LIUNA's Buffalo chapter, Local 210, had been controlled by the Mafia for decades.

In order to clean up Local 210, LIUNA appointed a trustee in February 1996 to oversee the chapter. Local members strongly resisted the trustee's appointment. For the first month some members prevented him from entering the local headquarters. Within two years, however, the trustee had expelled more than twenty local members for Mafia corruption. He also reformed local policies to ensure fair treatment of members. In December 1999 the Justice Department appointed another overseer, a court liaison officer, to help in the cleanup effort.

Within five years federal oversight and reforms had taken Local 210 out of the Mafia's hands. It was a major blow to the Buffalo crime family. They lost union jobs and control. For the first time in five years, Local 210 held free elections and was returned to member control.

A few days before the civil racketeering trial began, the Teamsters settled with the government. They signed a public confession that the Mafia controlled important parts of the union. The agreement outlawed members from racketeering or associating with Mafia members. It set up a court-supervised Independent Review Board to investigate and remove corrupt union officials. The agreement also directed that top union officials would be directly elected by the regular members in a secret ballot. A federally appointed overseer would oversee the elections and other union operations.

As the federal government booted out more than one hundred corrupt union officials, the union members applauded. One longtime member wrote: "Finally we are going to get rid of the hideous influence of organized crime. . . . Many besides myself would like to look you in the eye, shake your hand, pat you on the back, and say we really appreciate your effort."[68]

Like the Teamster case, the government has used RICO laws against several major unions and their local chapters. If investigators proved that local leaders were connected to the Mafia, the government removed them and placed the union under a trustee's control. The government also banned anyone with mob connections from being employed by the union or holding a union office. "There was a time that La Cosa Nostra could have shut down the United States through the control of labor unions. The key factor in their decline has been their removal in large measure from the Big Four labor unions,"[69] said Jim E. Moody, former deputy assistant director of the FBI's organized crime units.

The Pizza Connection Case

In the 1960s and 1970s, several pizza shops in the Northeast and Midwest did more than make pizza. These pizza shops served as a front for a huge Mafia heroin smuggling ring. Carmine Galante, Bonanno family boss at the time, worked with Sicilian Mafia members known as "zips" to run the operation. According to one Bonanno family member: "The zips

are Sicilians brought into this country to distribute heroin. They set up pizza parlors, where they received and distributed heroin, laundered money."[70] The Sicilians ran the heroin operation and gave the American mobsters a cut of the profits.

In 1979 gunmen shot Galante while he ate lunch at a New York restaurant. Investigators suspected that a power struggle between Galante and other members of the Bonanno family and the Commission triggered the murder. During the investigation, agents became suspicious of Galante's two bodyguards, zips who had escaped the shoot-out without a scratch. Surveillance of one bodyguard, Cesare Bonventre, revealed his connection to a pizzeria he owned with another Sicilian, Salvatore Catalano. The investigation of the two men uncovered the heroin operation.

For the next five years, investigators doggedly gathered evidence against the heroin smuggling ring. During that time they used fifty-five thousand wiretaps. They also gathered evidence from surveillance teams and tips from informants.

In the 1960s and 1970s, several pizza shops in the Northeast and Midwest served as a front for a huge Mafia heroin smuggling ring.

Undercover FBI agent Joseph Pistone, working as Donnie Brasco in the Bonanno family, also provided evidence against the Pizza Connection. By 1984 investigators had enough evidence to make arrests.

In April 1984 FBI agents arrested members of the Pizza Connection throughout the Northeast and Midwest. They named thirty-four defendants, although only twenty-two would be available for trial. The others were already in jail on other charges, on the run, or murdered before they could face trial. The defendants were charged with smuggling large amounts of heroin and cocaine into the United States and laundering the drug money. They were also charged under the RICO statute with conspiracy and the crime of managing a criminal enterprise. The two main defendants were leaders in the drug smuggling ring, Gaetano Badalamenti and Salvatore Catalano.

The scope of the case was staggering. Prosecutors traced an elaborate money-laundering operation that had transferred

Tommaso Buscetta, key informant in the Pizza Connection trial, appears during a court hearing in 1984.

more than $50 million to secret overseas bank accounts. Federal authorities claimed the smuggling ring had brought 1,650 pounds (748kg) of heroin into the United States since 1979. The drugs were worth a colossal $1.6 billion on the street. Attorney general William French Smith said the bust was "the most significant case involving heroin trafficking by traditional organized crime that has ever been developed by the Government."[71]

The Pizza Connection trial began in 1985 and lasted seventeen months. No drugs were seized, so lead prosecutor Louis Freeh had to rely on other evidence to prove his case. He knew that mountains of electronic eavesdropping transcripts ran the risk of being too dull for jury members. To solve that problem, Freeh hired professional actors to read the transcripts aloud and bring them to life. Freeh also brought in veteran narcotics agents to explain the meaning of different drug code words used in the transcripts.

In addition to the transcripts, a parade of witnesses testified against the defendants. Damaging testimony came from Mafia informants Tommaso Buscetta and Salvatore Contomo, who described the Mafia and its part in drug dealing.

In his closing argument to the jury, Freeh said:

> These 19 defendants, along with their co-conspirators who are not on trial, agreed and conspired to work as narcotics racketeers in order to generate millions of dollars. . . . Don't let yourself be intimidated by the length of this case. The proof here has been long and extensive, and you have listened to it with remarkable patience. . . . When it's all said and done, the case before you is about two commodities—dollars and drugs.[72]

After six days of deliberations, the jury found all but one defendant guilty. This time there would be no light jail sentences. Ten defendants received twenty to thirty-five years in jail. The others were sentenced to twelve to thirty-five years.

CHAPTER 6

Prosecution and Jail

When investigators feel they have gathered enough evidence against a Mafia criminal, they give the case to a prosecutor. Prosecutors are attorneys who bring the evidence together into a trial. They wade through mountains of paperwork, photographs, and surveillance tapes. It may be tedious work, but it is critical to building a successful case against the Mafia.

Organizing the Evidence

If the case is small, one attorney may handle the prosecution. In bigger Mafia cases, however, a team of prosecutors tackles the work together. To prepare for trial the prosecutors study their evidence inside and out. When John Kroger was a rookie assistant U.S. attorney in the Eastern New York District, his supervisor, Valerie Caproni, asked him to join the team prosecuting mobster Gregory Scarpa Jr. "I asked her if I could pick up the file," he said. Caproni laughed. "The Scarpa file fills fifteen filing cabinets,"[73] she replied.

Prosecutors comb through evidence, listening to surveillance tapes, reading transcripts, and watching videos. Many times that evidence is not well organized when prosecutors receive it. For the Scarpa case, evidence had been collected over ten years from wiretaps, bugs, video surveillance, tailing, subpoenas, garbage searches, and raids. It filled a windowless room known as the Scarpa War Room. Newly assigned to the case, Kroger and his coprosecutor discovered the room was a disaster. Kroger recalled:

> File cabinets and boxes had been packed so deeply against the walls I could not even locate a light switch. They rose

in perilous piles all the way to the ceiling. . . . Every time I tore open a box, I had no idea what I would find. In the first half hour, I uncovered hundreds of wiretap tapes, several pairs of scales for weighing cocaine and heroin, and stacks of old NYPD crime scene photos, pictures of Scarpa's victims.[74]

Kroger spent a week working in the war room, starting in the early morning and not leaving until late at night. Eventually his team decided to use almost one thousand pieces of evidence from the war room.

John Kroger, former assistant U.S. attorney in New York, joined the prosecuting team against Gregory Scarpa Jr. and had the daunting task of reviewing a roomful of evidence that had been collected over the last ten years.

Often prosecutors organize the key evidence elements into spreadsheets and charts that may be used in court. Sometimes prosecutors decide they need more evidence to prove a particular point. They will talk to investigators and send them out to collect the needed information.

Informants and Witnesses

Prosecutors also interview informants and other witnesses. Many times the prosecutors travel to meet with witnesses and prepare them for the trial. They run through scripted trial questions so the witnesses can feel as if they are in court.

Not every witness is good for the case. If they appear untrustworthy, they may hurt the case in the jury's eyes. "Prosecutors frequently have to make tough judgments about the value of witnesses, cutting their losses if a witness's baggage outweighs his potential contribution,"[75] says Kroger.

Many times prosecutors cannot rely directly on information from mob informants. Informants who are criminals might lie to save their own skin. In addition, a jury is more likely to believe an informant's testimony if other evidence supports it. Therefore, prosecutors like Ellen Corcella, a former assistant U.S. attorney in New York City, often try to verify informant information with other evidence. In one of Corcella's cases, Carmine Sessa, a consigliere in the Colombo crime family, decided to cooperate and tell investigators the location of a murder victim. "He said they buried the victim in the backroom of a particular store. About ten years later, they decided to dig up the body and dispose of it in another way,"[76] said Corcella.

To prove Sessa's statement was true, Corcella obtained a search warrant for the store. Police dug up the store floor. Apparently, the mobsters had been in a hurry when they moved the body, because they accidentally cut off pieces of the victim's fingers during the move. During the search, the police found the left-behind digits and Styrofoam cups the mobsters had tossed into the pit. Corcella brought in forensic geologists to

Becoming a Prosecutor

Job Description:
Prosecutors lead the trial against a criminal in court. Before the trial, prosecutors develop a trial strategy, organize evidence, and interview witnesses. They help investigators obtain search warrants and approvals for electronic surveillance. During a trial, prosecutors present the government's case against the defendant. Prosecutors can also be involved in negotiating a plea bargain and sentencing terms with defendants. Their caseload is often heavy, but a prosecutor's reward is obtaining justice for the American people.

Education:
After earning a four-year college degree, a prosecutor must complete three years of law school. Then the aspiring prosecutor must pass his or her state's bar exam to receive a law license.

Qualifications:
Many prosecutor jobs require applicants to have a few years of legal experience, preferably trial experience. Prosecutors spend much of their time in court, making trial skills an important part of the job.

Additional Information
In addition to legal experience, a good prosecutor must be sensitive to the community's needs. A prosecutor uses his or her judgment to know when to pursue a case, accept a plea bargain, or accept lesser charges. These decisions should be in the interest of justice, not a prosecutor's desire to punish a specific individual. In addition, a prosecutor must have excellent communication skills. He or she needs to be able to talk effectively with all types of people, including witnesses, police officers, victims, and judges.

Salary:
Salaries vary by location. In general, starting salaries range from $25,000 to $55,000. Experienced prosecutors can earn more than $100,000.

analyze the layers of concrete and dirt. The physical evidence found at the scene as well as the geologists' testimony both confirmed that Sessa had told the truth.

Preparing the Case

Using the evidence, prosecutors create a trial strategy. They decide what evidence and witnesses to use in court and the order in which to present the case. If a case has several prosecutors, the team decides which person will handle each part of the case in court. The prosecutor also tries to figure out what the defense's strategy will be. His or her team prepares its evidence to dispute any claims the defense will make.

During the course of a trial, the lead prosecutor is also responsible for making sure legal briefs are filed with the court. He or she coordinates the flow of information from investigators to the prosecutor's trial team and the defense's attorneys.

Bringing It All Together

In August 1983 Ronald Goldstock, director of New York State's Organized Crime Task Force, arrived in Manhattan for a meeting with the new U.S. attorney for the Southern District of New York, Rudolph Giuliani. "You came in just at the right time," Goldstock said to Giuliani. "We have the Corallo tapes and the FBI has tapes on the Colombos, Gambinos, and Genovese. You can bring a RICO case against the entire Commission—the Commission is the enterprise."[77] Giuliani agreed. He had read Joseph Bonanno's autobiography that year. "Bonanno has an entire section devoted to the Commission . . . if he could write about it, we could prosecute it,"[78] Giuliani said.

Giuliani and his staff spent months building an airtight RICO case against the Commission. He worked closely with the FBI and lead agent Pat Marshall. Marshall was responsible for reviewing and going through the evidence gathered by the different FBI crime squads. He gathered incriminating segments from bugged conversations and sifted through thousands of reports on the main suspects. When there was a hole in the evidence, Marshall dug deeper to fill it.

Commission Arrests

On February 25, 1985, federal agents swooped in and arrested one of the biggest hauls of Mafia bosses, underbosses, and leaders in history. Although all five New York bosses were included in the case, only three went to trial—Anthony Salerno, head of the Genovese family; Carmine Persico, head of the Colombo family; and Anthony Corallo, head of the Lucchese family. Paul Castellano, head of the Gambino family, was murdered before the trial began. The fifth boss, Philip "Rusty" Rastelli, head of

Anthony "Fat Tony" Salerno is released on bail February 26, 1985, after one of the biggest busts of Mafia bosses in history.

the Bonanno family, was dropped from the case and convicted in a separate RICO case. Other defendants included Gennaro Langella, a Colombo underboss; Salvatore Santoro, a Lucchese underboss; Christopher Furnari, a Lucchese consigliere; Ralph Scopo, a Colombo soldier; and Anthony Indelicato, a Bonanno hit man.

Assistant U.S. attorney Michael Chertoff led the government's prosecution. He would later become the secretary of homeland security under President George W. Bush. The Commission case was one of the first real courtroom tests of the RICO laws. Prosecutors knew that if they won convictions, the defense would appeal. The appellate courts could throw out the convictions if they found the RICO laws unconstitutional. It was a risk prosecutors were willing to take.

Chertoff's team knew that to win the case, they would have to convince the jurors of four facts. First, the Mafia and the Commission existed as entities. Second, the defendants were in fact members of the Commission or had followed its orders. Third, the Commission called for the murder of former Bonanno boss Carmine Galante. Fourth, the Commission controlled the concrete building industry in New York through extortion. The crimes of murder and extortion were the case's pattern of racketeering.

Commission Trial Begins

The Commission trial began in September 1986. In an unusual move, the jurors in the case were anonymous. Their identities and addresses were secret so that the defendants could not intimidate or tamper with them.

Chertoff and his team presented a mountain of evidence against the defendants. Some of the core pieces of evidence were the various tapes recorded through electronic surveillance.

The jury heard recordings in which defendants discussed the Commission. On one tape, Anthony Salerno talked to two members of the Cleveland family. When they asked for help in resolving a leadership dispute, Salerno told them he would pass along their requests to the Commission. "Let the Commission decide. Tell him it's the Commission from New York. Tell him he's dealing with the big boys now,"[79] Salerno said on the tape. The bug in the Lucchese Jaguar provided evidence about the scheduling of Commission meetings, a boss's power, and induction of members into the family.

An empty witness chair sits inside an American courtroom. During the course of the Commission trial, eighty-five witnesses were heard, and the jury convicted the defendants on every charge.

Murder in New Orleans

The first major Mafia incident in the United States occurred in New Orleans. Police chief David Hennessy was reportedly investigating Mafia violence and corruption in the city. In October 1890 Hennessy was gunned down in an execution-style murder. The way Hennessy died matched the Mafia custom of killing government officials who dared to cross them. Reports say that he fingered the Italian Mafia with his dying words.

Hennessy's killing provoked strong anti-Italian feelings in the New Orleans community. Police arrested hundreds of Sicilians. Nineteen were indicted for Hennessy's murder. After a jury acquitted several defendants, rumors of bribery and witness intimidation spread. In response an angry lynch mob stormed the jail and killed eleven of the nineteen defendants. The violence made headlines across the country. Although the defendants were never proven Mafia members, the Hennessy murder is believed to be the first major Mafia incident on American soil.

An illustration depicts the Mafia's intimidating of a New Orleans jury during the murder trial of police chief David Hennessey.

Testimony from informants like Cleveland mobster Angelo Lonardo added details and corroborated the taped conversations. Joseph Pistone, the FBI undercover agent who posed as Bonanno family associate Donnie Brasco, took the stand to testify about the Commission. Still, it was the words from their own mouths that most damaged the defendants.

To prove the Commission's control over the building industry, two contractors testified. The witnesses swore under oath that they had been forced to participate in the extortion scheme. One contractor testified that defendant Ralph Scopo, Colombo soldier and president of the concrete workers' union, informed him of the scheme. He would have to pay 2 percent of each concrete contract to the mobsters. "He [Scopo] said that it was going into a pot and would be divided among the families," testified the contractor. If he refused to pay, Scopo promised serious union trouble. "I don't think I had much of a choice,"[80] said the contractor.

Prosecutors presented forensic evidence that Anthony "Bruno" Indelicato, Colombo soldier, was involved in Carmine Galante's murder. They lifted a palm print from the gunmen's getaway car that matched Indelicato's print. To link the murder to the Commission, the prosecutors played a videotape of Indelicato being greeted and congratulated by Gambino underboss Aniello Dellacroce and Bonanno consigliere Stefano Cannone shortly after the murder. Prosecutors argued that the Commission had ordered the hit. When Indelicato carried it out, he rushed to report his success to his supervisors. Chertoff also pointed out that Indelicato was promoted to capo shortly after the murder, a typical reward for good service.

During the course of the trial, Chertoff's team called a staggering eighty-five witnesses. They played more than one hundred audiotapes and videotapes. They also showed countless surveillance photographs.

The defendants and their lawyers quickly realized their chances of beating the indictment were slim. The defense lawyers decided to try an unusual tactic. They admitted in open court that the Mafia and the Commission existed. "This case is not about whether there is a Mafia. Assume it. Accept it. There is. Nevertheless, just because a person is a member of the Mafia doesn't mean he has committed the charged crime or even agreed to commit the charged crime,"[81] argued defense attorney Samuel Dawson. Because the bosses did not make the admission themselves, they technically did not break their vow of *omerta*. Instead the lawyers did it for them.

Chertoff presented the government's closing argument:

> Merely the fact that a person is a member of the Mafia does not make him guilty of the crimes. But, part of the crime charged here is being part of the Mafia and part of the Commission of La Cosa Nostra. That is one of the elements, that is one half of the crimes, because the crime that is charged here is racketeering and what racketeering is about is setting up, joining, and associating with a criminal enterprise, organized crime activity, and using that organization to commit crimes like extortion and murder and loan sharking. . . . It is the Mafia that makes possible this kind of concerted criminal activity.[82]

After six days of deliberation, the jury convicted the defendants on every charge. The sentences were harsh. The three bosses, the underbosses, and Scopo received the maximum RICO sentence—one hundred years in jail without parole. Indelicato got a somewhat lighter sentence—forty years for the Galante murder. Appeals to higher courts upheld the verdicts.

The Commission case was a breakthrough for prosecutors. It provided a map for other Mafia cases to follow. The Commission case showed how to use the law effectively against the Mafia.

John Gotti, the Teflon Don

Unfortunately, in other cases the outcome was not as successful. Once arrested, hardened Mafia defendants are willing to

Mafia boss John Gotti was brought to court multiple times only to be acquitted because he intimidated and bribed witnesses. He was finally found guilty on multiple counts, including murder, in 1992.

do anything to avoid conviction. Gambino boss John Gotti was no exception. In fact, in 1984 Gotti roughed up a motorist on a Queens, New York, street and robbed him. When the angry victim reported the incident, police arrested Gotti for assault and theft. The motorist was the key witness in the case. During the trial, however, he was unable to remember the events with Gotti. Prosecutors suspected that Gotti intimidated or bribed the witness to change his story. The judge dismissed the case.

In 1985 Gotti faced RICO charges. Assistant U.S. attorney Diane Giacalone tried to link Gotti to extortion payments, murder, and armored car thefts. The case turned into a disaster when Gotti convinced a key witness not to testify. He also had an associate slip a bribe to one of the jurors to buy his vote. In the end the jury acquitted Gotti.

Eventually prosecutors learned from earlier mistakes and built a new case against Gotti. They arrested him again in 1990, on multiple charges of racketeering, extortion, jury tampering, and other crimes. This time, the case was airtight. The FBI had bugged a room over a social club where Gotti held meetings. Unaware of the bugs, Gotti admitted on tape to several

Secret Meetings

At times a prosecutor might have to speak to witnesses or informants who are in the Witness Security Program. Some of these informants are serving time in special prisons that have segregation units. There the informants are kept safe and away from the general prison population. When a prosecutor has to meet with one of these informants, he or she flies to meet with them. The meeting takes place at a special site within the prison, so other inmates do not know the informant is talking to the government.

Sometimes the prosecutor has to talk to a witness in the Witness Security Program living in a secret location. The U.S. Marshals Service coordinates the meeting. The prosecutor and witness meet at a neutral site, usually in a place without a large Mafia presence. The U.S. marshals wait until the night before the meeting to inform the prosecutor where he or she will be going. This protects the witness from leaks. During the meeting the prosecutor only knows the witness under his or her old name. The witness's new name and identity are never revealed.

murders. Now his own words were used against him in court. The FBI was also able to flip his trusted underboss, Sammy the Bull Gravano, to provide additional evidence. In addition, the trial judge ordered that the jurors remain anonymous to prevent any further jury tampering.

This combination of strong evidence and jury protection worked. In 1992 the jury found Gotti guilty of multiple counts, including murder. "The don is covered with Velcro, and every charge stuck,"[83] said New York FBI chief Jim Fox.

Clean Hands

According to former prosecutor Ellen Corcella, integrity is the single most important thing a prosecutor brings to a Mafia trial. "The jury has to believe and respect you. You are putting witnesses on the stand that are criminals themselves. You have to have a level of integrity that they [the jury] can respond to. If the jury thinks someone on the trial team is not on the up and up—it's not good,"[84] Corcella says.

Corcella knows firsthand the importance of a clean image. She lost several cases because an FBI agent's conduct crossed the line. During the 1980s FBI Special Agent Lindley "Lin" DeVecchio recruited Colombo mobster Gregory Scarpa Sr. as a mob informant. Scarpa agreed to provide details about the Colombo family and their crimes. In return DeVecchio agreed to give Scarpa legal protection. He knew that his informant was involved in many different crimes but decided to look the other way as long as Scarpa passed him good inside information.

Eventually DeVecchio's conduct crossed the line. He began to slip confidential information to Scarpa. It was believed that he tipped off Scarpa about the potential hiding places of his enemies during the Colombo family war in the early 1990s.

> **By the Numbers**
>
> **$60,000**
>
> **Amount of money John Gotti paid a juror to vote for his acquittal**

He was also suspected of passing along information about pending arrests, surveillance, informants, and rivals. Eventually Scarpa got as much valuable information from DeVecchio as he gave.

In one of Corcella's 1995 trials, defense lawyers for seven Colombo family defendants shone a spotlight on the relationship between Scarpa and DeVecchio. The defendants, including brothers Victor M. and John Orena, were charged with conspiracy to commit murder and carrying firearms. Defense lawyers claimed that their clients were simply acting in self-defense against Scarpa and his allies. They also argued that DeVecchio's actions protected Scarpa and aided him in the Colombo family war.

Corcella tried to get the jury to ignore the issue of DeVecchio's conduct. "Don't be distracted or detoured by Scarpa. You are not here to determine if Agent DeVecchio was incompetent or guilty . . . or if Scarpa compromised DeVecchio," she told the jury. "He'll get his day in court,"[85] she added.

Her argument fell on deaf ears. The jury acquitted all seven defendants. After the trial, jurors said they had been influenced by the defense's argument that DeVecchio had encouraged the family war and the defendant's actions were in self-defense against Scarpa.

Behind Bars

Before heavy RICO sentences, the Mafia viewed prison time as a regular part of life. Members could do a few years, and then jump back into family life when they got out of jail. Some families continued to operate with temporary leaders, knowing the jailed mafioso would be back in a short time. Others ran family business from inside prison. They used lawyers or family members to get messages out to trusted associates.

While serving time for a drug conviction, Colombo family capo Gregory Scarpa Jr. continued to collect his share of profits from family businesses. From jail he ordered a murder on the street. He planned his return while his father rebuilt

their crew, replacing jailed associates with fresh, tough men. Scarpa sent this message to his team: "Stay tough. We will all be together again soon."[86]

Under RICO sentences, the promise of reuniting with the Mafia family has faded. Many bosses and other leaders serve decades and even life behind bars. For the first time the major families are in turmoil while much of their leadership sits in prison.

Future of the Mafia

Despite the recent success in Mafia investigations and prosecutions, some experts warn that the Mafia is ready and able to regroup and resurface. Since the attacks of September 11, 2001, the FBI's attention has been focused on terrorist threats. Some experts warn that leaving the Mafia alone even when they are down and hurting is a critical mistake. The FBI learned this lesson the hard way in the past. When they took the pressure off a weakened Bonanno family in the 1980s, Joe Massino built the Bonannos back into a powerful crime family. "The lesson we learned is that you cannot deemphasize vigilance on any of the families. All are capable of comebacks,"[87] said former FBI agent Bruce Mouw.

New York police lieutenant Remo Franceschini agrees. "In the old days, back in Sicily, they would say, 'We're going back to the caves.' They would go back to the caves to protect themselves and regroup. That's what I expect the Mob will do."[88]

Notes

Introduction: La Cosa Nostra

1. Quoted in George Anastasia, *The Last Gangster*. New York: Harper-Collins, 2004, p. 19.
2. Quoted in Anastasia, *The Last Gangster*, p. 19.
3. Quoted in Anastasia, *The Last Gangster*, p. 19.
4. Quoted in Selwyn Raab, *Five Families: The Rise, Decline, and Resurgence of America's Most Powerful Mafia Empires*. New York: St. Martin's, 2005. p. 698.

Chapter 1: Knowing the Enemy

5. Quoted in Raab, *Five Families*, p. 20.
6. Quoted in Raab, *Five Families*, p. 24.
7. Quoted in Selwyn Raab, "In the Mafia, Too, a Decline in Standards," *New York Times*, January 19, 1992. www.nytimes.com/1992/01/19/week inreview/in-the-mafia-too-a-decline-in-standards.html.
8. Quoted in Raab, *Five Families*, p. 3.
9. Quoted in Elizabeth Neuffer and Kevin Cullen, "FBI Tapes Offer a Rare Inside Look at Mafia Induction," *Boston Globe*, March 27, 1990. www.thelaborers.net/lexisnexis/articles/fbi_tapes_offer_a_rare_inside_look.htm.
10. Quoted in Neuffer and Cullen, "FBI Tapes Offer a Rare Inside Look at Mafia Induction."
11. Quoted in Neuffer and Cullen, "FBI Tapes Offer a Rare Inside Look at Mafia Induction."
12. Quoted in Peter Maas, *The Valachi Papers*. New York: Putnam's Sons, 1968, p. 96.
13. Quoted in Jerry Capeci, *The Complete Idiot's Guide to the Mafia*. New York: Alpha, 2004, p. 27.
14. Jim Turner, interview with the author, July 6, 2009.
15. Quoted in Federal Bureau of Investigation, "Italian Organized Crime—Overview." www.fbi.gov/hq/cid/org crime/lcnindex.htm.
16. U.S. Department of Labor, "The OIG's Labor Racketeering Program." www.oig.dol.gov/laborracprogram.htm.
17. Quoted in Raab, *Five Families*, p. 34.

Chapter 2: Mafia Fighters

18. John Kroger, *Convictions: A Prosecutor's Battles Against Mafia Killers,*

Drug Kingpins and Enron Thieves. New York: Farrar, Straus and Giroux, 2009, p. 140.

19. Joe Griffin and Don DeNevi, *Mob Nemesis: How the FBI Crippled Organized Crime.* Amherst, NY: Prometheus, 2002, p. 65.

20. Ellen Corcella, interview with the author, July 9, 2009.

21. Griffin and DeNevi, *Mob Nemesis*, pp. 70–71.

22. Griffin and DeNevi, *Mob Nemesis*, pp. 71–72.

23. Griffin and DeNevi, *Mob Nemesis*, pp. 71-72.

24. Office of the Attorney General—State of New York, "About the Organized Crime Task Force." www.oag .state.ny.us/bureaus/organized_crime /about.html.

25. Corcella, interview. July 9, 2009.

26. Quoted in Federal Bureau of Investigation, "Considered a Career as an FBI Language Specialist?" www.fbi.gov/ page2/dec04/upclose 121704 .htm.

27. Quoted in Kevin Bohn and Kelli Arena, "Mafia Feels Heat from Feds, Crime Rivals," CNN, July 16, 2008. www.cnn.com/2008/CRIME/07/ 16/fbi.mob/index.html.

28. Quoted in Raab, *Five Families*, p. 647.

29. Quoted in Raab, *Five Families*, p. 265.

30. Corcella, interview.

31. Quoted in Department of Justice, "Sixty-two Defendants Indicted, Including Gambino Organized Crime Family Acting Boss, Acting Underboss, Consigliere, and Members and Associates, as Well as Construction Industry and Union Officials," press release, Federal Bureau of Investigation —New York, February 7, 2008. http:// newyork.fbi.gov/dojpressrel/pressrel 08/organizedcrime020708 .htm.

Chapter 3: Surveillance

32. Griffin and DeNevi, *Mob Nemesis*, p. 63.

33. Quoted in Dina Temple-Raston, "FBI Surveillance Team Reveals Tricks of the Trade," National Public Radio, July 5, 2008. www.npr.org/ templates/story/story.php?storyId= 92207687.

34. Quoted in Temple-Raston, "FBI Surveillance Team Reveals Tricks of the Trade."

35. Quoted in Temple-Raston, "FBI Surveillance Team Reveals Tricks of the Trade."

36. Quoted in Temple-Raston, "FBI Surveillance Team Reveals Tricks of the Trade."

37. Quoted in Temple-Raston, "FBI Surveillance Team Reveals Tricks of the Trade."

38. Quoted in Joseph D. Pistone and Richard Woodley, *Donnie Brasco: My Undercover Life in the Mafia*. New York: New American Library, 1987, p. 117.

39. Quoted in Ed Magnuson, "Hitting the Mafia," *Time*, June 24, 2001. www.time.com/time/magazine/article /0,9171,145082,00.html.

40. Quoted in Raab, *Five Families*, p. 623.

41. Pistone and Woodley, *Donnie Brasco*, p. 105.

Chapter 4: Inside Information

42. Quoted in Bohn and Arena, "Mafia Feels Heat from Feds, Crime Rivals."

43. Griffin and DeNevi, *Mob Nemesis*, p. 111.

44. Griffin and DeNevi, *Mob Nemesis*, p. 71.

45. Quoted in Raab, *Five Families*, p. 211.

46. Quoted in Thomas Reppetto, *Bringing Down the Mob: The War Against the American Mafia*. New York: Henry Holt, 2006, p. 130.

47. Quoted in Reppetto, *Bringing Down the Mob*, p. 130.

48. Quoted in Federal Bureau of Investigation, "The Case of the Stuffed Canary," July 6, 2004. www.fbi.gov/ page2/july04/canary070604.htm.

49. Quoted in Federal Bureau of Investigation, "The Case of the Stuffed Canary."

50. Quoted in Maas, *The Valachi Papers*, p. 59.

51. Quoted in Maas, *The Valachi Papers*, p. 28.

52. Quoted in Maas, *The Valachi Papers*, pp. 31–32.

53. Quoted in Maas, *The Valachi Papers*, p. 37.

54. Quoted in Raab, *Five Families*, p. 435.

55. Quoted in Capeci, *The Complete Idiot's Guide to the Mafia*, p. 267.

56. Quoted in Raab, *Five Families*, p. 453.

57. Quoted in Capeci, *The Complete Idiot's Guide to the Mafia*, p. 273.

58. Pistone and Woodley, *Donnie Brasco*, p. 97.

59. Pistone and Woodley, *Donnie Brasco*, p. 98.

60. Pistone and Woodley, *Donnie Brasco*, p. 57.

61. Quoted in Pistone and Woodley, *Donnie Brasco*, p. 367.

62. Pistone and Woodley, *Donnie Brasco*, p. 371.

Chapter 5: RICO and the Law

63. Quoted in Raab, *Five Families*, p. 217.

64. Quoted in Raab, *Five Families*, p. 217.

65. Quoted in Pistone and Woodley, *Donnie Brasco*, p. 186.

66. Angelo Lonardo, "Statement of Angelo Lonardo Before the U.S. Senate Subcommittee on Investigations," *Nevada Observer*, April 9, 2006. www.nevadaobserver.com/Reading %20Room%20Documents/Cleveland %20LCN%20-Statement%20of %20Angelo%20Lonardo%20(1988) .htm.

67. Quoted in Capeci, *The Complete Idiot's Guide to the Mafia*, p. 246.

68. Quoted in Eugene H. Methvin, "The Liberation of the Teamsters," *National Review*, March 30, 1992. http:// findarticles.com/p/articles/mi_m12 82/is_n6_v44/ai_12111793.

69. Quoted in Capeci, *The Complete Idiot's Guide to the Mafia*, p. 262.

70. Quoted in Mike La Sorte, "Gaetano Badalamenti and the Pizza Connection," American Mafia, July 2004. www.americanmafia.com/Feature_ Articles_271.html.

71. Quoted in Arnold H. Lubash, "17 Found Guilty in 'Pizza' Trial of a Drug Ring," *New York Times*, March 3, 1987. www.nytimes.com/1987/03/ 03/nyregion/17-found-guilty-in- pizza-trial-of-a-drug-ring.html? scp=5&sq=pizza %20 connection%20 trial&st=cse& pagewanted=2.

72. Quoted in H. Lubash, "Summations Begin in the 'Pizza Connection' Trial," *New York Times*, January 28, 1987. www.nytimes.com/1987/01/28/nyreg ion/summations-begin-in-the-pizza- connection-trial.html? scp=2&sq= pizza%20=connection%20trial&st=cse.

Chapter 6: Prosecution and Jail

73. Quoted in Kroger, *Convictions*, p. 128.

74. Kroger, *Convictions*, p. 159.

75. Kroger, *Convictions*, p. 162.

76. Corcella, interview.

77. Quoted in Raab, *Five Families*, p. 256.

78. Quoted in Magnuson, "Hitting the Mafia."

79. Quoted in Raab, *Five Families*, p. 278.

80. Quoted in Raab, *Five Families*, p. 285.

81. Quoted in Magnuson, "Hitting the Mafia."

82. Quoted in Raab, *Five Families*, pp. 297–98.

83. Quoted in Capeci, *The Complete Idiot's Guide to the Mafia*, p. 299.

84. Corcella, interview.

85. Quoted in Selwyn Raab, "7 Suspects Say F.B.I. Agent Helped Incite Mob Murders," *New York Times*, May 10, 1995. www.nytimes.com/1995/05/ 10/nyregion/7-suspects-say-fbi-agent -helped-incite-mob-murders.html?

scp=1&sq=ellen%20corcella%20persico&st=cse.

86. Quoted in Kroger, *Convictions*, p. 144.

87. Quoted in Raab, *Five Families*, p. 699.

88. Quoted in Raab, *Five Families*, p. 708.

Glossary

acquitted: Found not guilty beyond a reasonable doubt.

bribe: Money or other valuable item given to someone in order to influence his or her behavior.

convicted: Found guilty of a crime.

Cosa Nostra: A name for the Mafia that means "our thing" in Italian.

defendant: The person accused of a crime in a criminal trial.

evidence: Information presented in testimony or in documents that is used to persuade the judge or jury.

fence: To receive or sell stolen goods; also, a person who receives stolen goods.

induction: An initiation ceremony.

informant: A person who gives information, usually in secret.

intelligence: The gathering of information.

mafioso: A member of the Mafia.

mole: An undercover agent working inside a criminal group like the Mafia.

oath: A solemn promise.

prosecutor: An attorney who tries a criminal case on behalf of the government.

racket: An organized illegal activity.

sentence: A defendant's punishment when convicted of a crime.

statute: A law passed by a legislature.

subpoena: A court order to obtain witnesses, records, or documents.

surveillance: A watch kept over a person, group, or location.

testimony: Oral evidence presented by witnesses during trials or before grand juries.

witness: A person called upon by either side in a trial to give testimony before the court or jury.

For More Information

Books

Michael Benson, *Criminal Investigations: Organized Crime*. New York: Infobase, 2008. Overview of organized crime, including the Mafia.

Jerry Capeci, *The Complete Idiot's Guide to the Mafia*. New York: Alpha, 2004. Excellent overview of the Mafia, its operations, and history.

Selwyn Raab, *Five Families: The Rise, Decline, and Resurgence of America's Most Powerful Mafia Empires*. New York: St. Martin's, 2005. Exhaustive history of the five major New York Mafia families.

Internet Source

New York Daily News, "Rats! Mob Informants," December 18, 2009. www .nydailynews.com/news/ny_crime/ galleries/rats_mob_informants/rats_m ob_informants.html#ph0.

Web Sites

Federal Bureau of Investigation— Organized Crime (www.fbi.gov/hq/ cid/orgcrime/ocshome.htm). This Web site gives the history and an overview of the FBI's investigation of the Mafia. It includes anecdotes of specific Mafia figures and cases, as well as information about working for the FBI.

United States Department of Justice— United States Attorneys (www.usdoj .gov/usao). This site provides information about the job of a U.S. attorney and includes a "Kids Page" to explain the role of U.S. attorneys.

Index

Picture Credits

About the Author

Carla Mooney received her undergraduate degree in economics from the University of Pennsylvania. She has written several books for young people, including *Bioethics* and *Online Social Networking*, which are part of Lucent Books' Hot Topics series.

Mooney lives with her husband and three children in Pittsburgh, Pennsylvania. When she is not writing, she also volunteers as the Pittsburgh chapter director for Flashes of Hope, a nonprofit organization that takes professional pictures of children with cancer and other life-threatening conditions.